Eyewitness Accounts of the American Revolution

New Travels Through North America
Abbé Robin

The New York Times & Arno Press

NEW TRAVELS

THROUGH

NORTH-AMERICA:

From the original Portrait in Col. Trumbull's Picture of the Surrender of Lord Cornwallis.
Painted from life at Paris in 1787.

D. C. Hinman Sc.

JEAN-BAPTISTE DONATIEN DE VIMEUR,

COMTE DE ROCHAMBEAU.

NEW TRAVELS

THROUGH

NORTH-AMERICA:

In a Series of LETTERS;

Exhibiting, the History of the Victorious Campaign of the Allied Armies, under his Excellency General Washington, and the Count de Rochambeau, in the Year 1781.

Interfperfed with political, and philofophical Obfervations, upon the genius, temper, and cuftoms of the AMERICANS; Alfo, Narrations of the capture of General BURGOYNE, and Lord CORNWALLIS, with their ARMIES; and a variety of interefting particulars, which occurred, in the courfe, of the

WAR in AMERICA.

TRANSLATED from the original of the Abbé ROBIN; one of the Chaplains to the French Army in AMERICA.

From fuch events, let boaftful Nations know,
Jove lays the pride of haughtieft Monarchs low,
And they, who kindled with ambitious fire,
In arts, and arms, with moft fuccefs afpire,
When turn'd to tyrants, but provoke their doom,
Grafp at their fate, and build themfelves a tomb.
                                    Busiris by Young.

PHILADELPHIA:

Printed and Sold by ROBERT BELL, in Third-Street.

M, DCC, LXXXIII.——*Price Two Thirds of a Dollar.* (1783)

VERSES on the PROSPECT of planting ARTS and LEARNING in AMERICA.

Written upwards of fifty years since, by the celebrated DIVINE,
and PHILOSOPHER, Dr. BERKELEY, Bishop of CLOYNE,
in IRELAND.

THE muse, disgusted at an age and clime,
　　Barren of every glorious theme,
In distant lands now waits a better time,
　　Producing subjects worthy fame :

In happy climes, where from the genial sun
　　And virgin earth such scenes ensue,
The force of art by nature seems outdone,
　　And fancied beauties by the true :

In happy climes, the seat of innocence,
　　Where NATURE guides and VIRTUE rules,
Where men shall not impose for truth and sense,
　　The pedantry of courts and schools :

There shall be sung another golden age,
　　The rise of EMPIRE and of ARTS;
The good and great inspiring epic rage,
　　The wisest heads and noblest hearts !

Not such as Europe breeds in her decay ;——
　　Such as she bred when fresh and young,
When heavenly flame did animate her clay,
　　By future poets shall be sung.

WESTWARD the star of empire takes its way ;
　　The four first acts already past,
A fifth shall close the Drama with the day ;——
　　Time's noblest offspring is the last.

INTRODUCTION.

IN the following Letters the reader will not meet with a dry relation of events merely military. The Author, avoiding the naked brevity and minute precifion of a camp Journal, occafionally adverts to the natural hiftory, and politics of America, as well as to the religion, national character, and cuftoms of the inhabitants.

Some pains have been taken, in this tranflation, to retain, if poffible, the ftyle and philofophical manner of the French original, which often deviates from the common line of fimple narration, and introduces fentiment as well as defcription.

The Author appears to be a philofopher, and though many of his ideas on religion, politics, genius of the people &c. may be diffonant from our mode of thinking on thefe points, in America, and fometimes perhaps really ill founded, yet there is certainly more fatisfaction in difcovering what opinion a foreigner entertains of us, although only from a cafual acquaintance, a tranfient vifit to the country, than in reading the beft accounts and narratives of our own, which, in fuch matters, may be fufpected of being too ready to humour our local prejudices, or flatter our vanity.

They who would faunter over half the Globe to copy the infcription on an antique column, to meafure the altitude of a pyramid, or defcribe the ornaments on the Grand Seignior's State Turban, will fcarcely find any thing in American Travels to gratify their tafte. The works of art are here comparatively trivial and inconfiderable, the fplendor of pageantry rather obfcure, and confequently few or none but the admirers of fimple Nature can either travel with pleafure themfelves

or

INTRODUCTION

or read the travels of others with fatisfaction, through this country.

Moft of thofe accounts of North-America, given to the public by Britifh explorers and others, previous to the Revolution, are generally taken up, with the recital of wonderful adventures, in the woods beyond the Lakes, or with the Hiftories and records of the wild Indian nations, fo that by the time the reader gets through one of thofe performances he never fails to be better acquainted with the *Ottagamies, Cherokees, Miamees, Nadouweffians,* and a hundred others, with their various cuftoms of *paw-wawing,* or methods of making *wampum,* than with the moft interefting particulars relative to the *inhabitants* of the *then* colonies; *thefe* were but rarely thought worth mentioning by thofe gentlemen, and when they are, it is mortifying enough to fee them conftantly confidered rather as mere beafts of burden, calculated folely for the fupport of the grandeur, wealth and omnipotence of Great Britain, than as men and Free-Men.

Our French Author is more liberal---two years before the prefent peace he confidered the United-States as a great independent nation, advancing with hafty ftrides to the fummit of power and fovereignty.

Concife, yet curious accounts of two of the greateft events that have happened in this or any other age, will be found in the following performance: thefe cannot fail of attracting fome fhare of the reader's attention, not only becaufe they were the vifible means of accelerating an independence, which, according to probability, and in the natural courfe of human affairs, was the tafk of another century, but alfo becaufe the philofophers both of America and of Europe, in confequence of the pacification thereby effected, have their ideas upon the ftretch, carefully anticipating the commercial, and political advantages, or difadvantages, refulting from this very extraordinary Revolution.

THE TRANSLATOR.

CONTENTS.

LETTER

CONTENTS.

LETTER

CONTENTS.

APPENDIX.

CONTENTS.

APPENDIX.

CONTAINING.

N. B. *This Circular Letter was directed, to each of the different Governors of the Thirteen United States, who are at present as follows.*

New-Hampshire, The Honourable,	Meshech Weare, Esquire.
Massachusetts,	John Hancock, Esquire.
Rhode-Island,	William Greene, Esquire.
Connecticut,	John Trumbull, Esquire.
New-York,	George Clinton, Esquire.
New-Jersey,	William Livingston, Esq.
Pennsylvania,	John Dickinson, Esquire.
Delaware,	Nicholas Van Dyke, Esq.
Maryland,	William Paca, Esquire.
Virginia,	Benjamin Harrison, Esq.
North Carolina,	Alexander Martin, Esquire.
South-Carolina,	Benjamin Guerard, Esquire.
Georgia,	Lyman Hall, Esquire.

NEW

NEW TRAVELS

THROUGH

NORTH-AMERICA.

LETTER I. *The Author's Voyage from France to America.—Arrival at Boston.—Boston and its Harbour.—Manners and customs of the inhabitants—of the Quakers, and remarks upon their mode of worship.—American Ladies.—Commerce of Boston.—Colleges at Cambridge.—American prejudices against the French Nation.—Arrival of Count Rochambeau and the French Army at Newport, in Rhode-Island.*

Boston June 24th. 1781.

I HAVE at length, my dear friend, accomplished my long Voyage over the vast Atlantic. For the space of no less than eighty five days we were tossed about in our floating habitation, but in the worst of our danger, and when we were seemingly upon the point of being overturned by the fury of the winds and waves, I had the satisfaction to find that our ship constantly returned to her original position by that universal all-pervading principle, the central attraction of gravity. How many efforts, how much time must it have taken to have perfected these huge and unwieldy machines, by the aid of which men are enabled to despise the utmost fury and most violent agitations of the waves! Like new *Eoluses* they curb the impetuosity of the winds, or by the power of reaction force them to contribute to the progress of the voyage, in almost opposite directions.

But alas! this noble art has not yet been able to secure the voyager from that disagreeable malady called *sea sickness*, occasioned by the motion of the vessel. I believe I have suffered as much from this nauseous complaint as any person that ever went to sea, and notwithstanding the frequent use of acids, it for a long time wholly

B

wholly prevented me from attending to any kind of bufinefs, or paying a particular attention to the many objects that furrounded me. Languifhing with weaknefs, and confined to the narrow bounds of this floating prifon, hearing nothing from morning till night but the barbarous phrafes peculiar to the fea and failors, I was in no condition to obferve or reflect upon the awful beauties of the ocean, or the grandeur of the fcene around me. With perfect indifference I beheld it toffing, boiling and foaming ; fwelling into mountains, or jumbled into a chaos of confufion ; its vapour exhaling into the air, or forming artificial rainbows about our veffel, while it at the fame time menaced us with deftruction. With little or no emotion, I faw it abate of its rage, grow fmooth, extend the limits of the horizon, and prefently refemble an immenfe mafs of oil, ftill however retaining its undulation. But it was difficult for me to withhold my attention from thofe fcintillations of light, which the moft inconfiderable motion in the water ftruck out of obfcurity ; they were particularly remarkable when a frefh gale drove the veffel through the water with an increafed rapidity ; fhe then feemed to plunge into torrents of flaming phofphorus, and to be making a tremendous progrefs through plains of liquid fire. I revolved in my own mind, what could be the caufe of this fingular, though common appearance, which I believe has never been thoroughly inveftigated :   Are they atoms of falt which, from their feveral furfaces, reflect the rays of light ?   Or is it their collifion with the fulphurous particles, that kindles them into flame, or are they rather the igneous fluid, the radical fire that is fuppofed to be the firft caufe of fluidity in the other elements ?

We fteered a foutherly courfe till we came to the 30th. degree of North Latitude.   The fea in this climate appeared to me to have more of a greenifh caft than before, and to abound throughout with this fire refembling phofphorus; we there faw the goldfifh, the voracious dolphin, and the flying fifh, which to efcape the former, flies out of the water, but falls down again as foon as the air has dried the moifture on its wings.   I did not know the galley fifh, tho' common enough on our coafts ; but the failors caught one, which I examined with the moft fcrupulous attention.   Nature has given it a bladder, which buoys it up and ferves as a rudder to direct its courfe; its whole contexture is nothing more than a flimy mafs, the organifation of which I had not time thoroughly to confider; it is provided with long fibres encircled with rings, which ferve to give it a hold in the water, fo as not to be driven away by the violence of the wind ; and through thefe fibres they alfo fuck up the food that ferves for their fubfiftence.   I touched this animal with my finger, and immediately had the painful fenfation of a burn, and forty-eight hours afterwards I ftill felt the effects of this penetrating cauftic.

In fine weather I ufed to take great pleafure, at night, in contemplating the grand profpect of the ftarry firmament over our heads; but the wonted order and regularity of the Heavens was

wholly

wholly altered; the ecliptic circle had withdrawn itſelf a great diſtance from the Horizon, the pole-ſtar had approached very near thereto, and the great Bear was about ſetting and concealing himſelf entirely from our view: what ſurpriſed me moſt, was, that the milky way had diſappeared, although I plainly perceived the conſtellation of the *Swan*, which is known to have its place in the midſt of it—I could wiſh the philoſophers would explain this aſtronomical myſtery, thoſe eſpecially who argue that the *Galaxy* is nothing more than an immenſe collection of ſtars; for why ſhould theſe ſtars diſappear, when all the reſt of the heavenly bodies are viſible here as well as in other places?———I now no longer wondered at the idea of the ancients about the riſing and ſetting of the ſun in the ocean:

Being often forced for the ſake of freſh air to be upon deck at the time of his appearing or diſappearing, I obſerved him ſome-times detaching himſelf ſlowly from the line that bounded the ſkies and waters, and at other times falling perpendicularly into the midſt of the waves; the eye, with a momentary deception, perſuading itſelf that the Horizon was plunging after the great luminary.——

The ſea, you well know, has plants and herbage peculiar to itſelf; it is remarkable that nature has formed them conſiderably different from land vegetables in colour, ſhape and properties; and if of a leſs delicate ſtructure, it was doubtleſs ordered ſo becauſe ſhe did not intend this element to produce animals as precious and ſo exquiſitely wrought as the other. The marine plants, however, are not without evident traces of the wiſe hand that formed them; I often ſaw the ſea covered with theſe ſaline herbs for a great ſpace, and in examining them, remarked among other things that inſtead of fibrous roots, they had parts ſomewhat like hands to attach themſelves to the rocks, a ſtem flatted at the end, and thick leaves, the better to refiſt the ſhock of the waves; and all provided at ſmall intervals with cells nearly empty of air, which by this means counterpoiſed their ſpecific weight, and forced them to tend con-ſtantly in a perpendicular direction toward the ſurface of the water.

I cannot give you a competent idea of the agreeable emotions I experienced at the ſight of land, which at firſt appeared like a thin miſt at the very extremity of the Horizon. What moment of life is comparable to that when a man is upon the point of re-enjoying his health, coming within reach of objects which intereſt the mind, the heart and the ſenſes, and finding, inſtead of a late chaos and the ghaſtly image of deſtruction, a world of nature every where organized into the moſt elegant ſymmetry and perfection—to walk upon the graſſy plain, to breathe the perfume of a thouſand flowers, to enjoy the ſhade of the trees, to liſten to the harmony of the birds of the grove, and to ſee them ſoar aloft and poiſe themſelves in the air!

It

It is abfence from thefe enjoyments that makes their value the better known, and that fwells the foul with gratitude to the benign creator of all, when we are reftored to them. A leafy branch floating on the furface of the water made my heart leap with joy, as this was the token of a new world ready to appear. We had now doubled Cape Anne and were at the mouth of the great Bay of Maffachufetts, could plainly perceive the waves breaking upon the rock of Cape Cod, and in a few hours might have been at Bofton, had not a thick fog fuddenly furrounded us, and left us at a lofs which way to fteer, being in the midft of fhoals and ledges: in this uncertainty we caft anchor, but foon after, a ftrong contrary wind drove us from our anchors, broke the cables, nearly forced feveral of our fhips foul of each other, and threatened us with inevitable fhipwreck in thefe very dangerous Latitudes.

The greater part of the veffels put before the wind and fteered from the land, defpairing of gaining this much defired port, but after two days of uncertainty and danger, a happy change of wind and weather brou ht us fafe into the Harbour of Bofton. From this road, which is interfperfed with feveral agreeable little Iflands, we difcovered through the woods, on the fide toward the weft, a magnificent profpect of houfes, built on a curved line, and extending afterwards in a femicircle above half a league—This was Bofton. Thefe edifices which were lofty and regular, with fpires and cupolas intermixt at proper diftances, did not feem to us a modern fettlement fo much as an ancient city, enjoying all the embellifhments and population, that never fail to attend on commerce and the arts.

The infide of the town does not at all leffen the idea that is formed by an exterior profpect: a fuperb wharf has been carried out above two thoufand feet into the fea, and is broad enough for ftores and work-fhops through the whole of its extent; it communicates at right angles with the principal ftreet of the town, which is both large and fpacious, and bends in a curve parallel to the harbour ; this ftreet is ornamented with elegant buildings, for the moft part two or three ftories high, and many other ftreets terminate in this, communicating with it on each fide. The form and conftruction of the houfes would furprife a European eye ; they are built of brick, and wood, not in the clumfy and melancholy tafte of our ancient European towns, but regularly and well provided with windows and doors. The wooden work or frame is light, covered on the outfide with thin boards, well plained, and lapped over each other as we do tiles on our roofs in France ; thefe buildings are generally painted with a pale white colour, which renders the profpect much more pleafing than it would otherwife be; the roofs are fet off with balconies, doubtlefs for the more ready extinguifhing of fire; the whole is fupported by a wall of about a foot high ; it is eafy to fee how great an advantage thefe houfes have over ours, in point of neatnefs and falubrity.

All the parts of thefe buildings are fo well joined, and their
weight

weight is fo equally divided, and proportionate to their bulk, that they may be removed from place to place with little difficulty.— I have feen one of two ftories high removed above a quarter of a mile, if not more, from its original fituation, and the whole French army have feen the fame thing done at Newport. What they tell us of the travelling habitations of the Scythians is far lefs wonderful. Their houfehold furniture is fimple, but made of choice wood, after the Englifh fafhion, which renders their appearance lefs gay: their floors are covered with handfome carpets, or painted cloths, but others fprinkle them with fine fand.

This city is fuppofed to contain about fix thoufand houfes, and thirty thoufand inhabitants; there are nineteen churches for the feveral fects here, all of them convenient, and feveral finifhed with tafte and elegance, efpecially thofe of the Prefbyterians and the Church of England; their form is generally a long fquare, ornamented with a pulpit, and furnifhed with pews of a fimilar fabrication throughout. The poor as well as the rich hear the word of God in thefe places in a convenient and decent pofture of body.

Sunday is obferved with the utmoft ftrictnefs; all bufinefs, how important foever, is then totally at a ftand, and the moft innocent recreations and pleafures prohibited. Bofton, that populous town, where at other times there is fuch a hurry of bufinefs, is on this day a mere defert; you may walk the ftreets without meeting a fingle perfon, and if by chance you meet one, you fcarcely dare to ftop and talk with him. A Frenchman that lodged with me took it into his head to play on the flute on Sundays for his amufement; the people upon hearing it were greatly enraged, collected in crowds round the houfe and would have carried matters to extremity in a fhort time with the mufician, had not the landlord given him warning of his danger, and forced him to defift. Upon this day of melancholy you cannot go into a houfe but you find the whole family employed in reading the Bible; and indeed it is an affecting fight to fee the father of a family furrounded by his houfhold, hearing him explain the fublime truths of this facred volume.

Nobody fails here of going to the place of worfhip appropriated to his fect. In thefe places there reigns a profound filence; an order and refpect is alfo obfervable which has not been feen for a long time in our Catholic churches. Their pfalmody is grave and majeftic, and the harmony of the Poetry, in their national tongue, adds a grace to the mufic, and contributes greatly towards keeping up the attention of the worfhippers.

All thefe churches are deftitute of ornaments. No addreffes are made to the heart and the imagination; there is no vifible object to fuggeft to the mind for what purpofe a man comes into thefe places, what he *is* and what he *will fhortly be*. Neither painting nor fculpture reprefent thofe great events which ought to recall him to his duty and awaken his gratitude, nor are thofe *heroes* in piety

brought

brought into view, whom it is his duty to admire and endeavour to imitate. The pomp of ceremony is here wanting to fhadow out the greatnefs of the *being* he goes to worfhip; there are no proceffions to teftify the homage we owe to *him*, that great Spirit of the Univerfe, by whofe will Nature itfelf exifts, through whom the fields are covered with harvefts, and the trees are loaded with fruits.

The Quakers, ftill greater enemies to outward ceremonies in worfhip, have banifhed from amongft them the very appearance of a priefthood: In vain will you look into their meeting houfes for a minifter particularly commiffioned to fpeak in the name of the Divinity. The eye can difcover nothing but a filent, meditating, melancholy affembly, collected together without any apparent motive or defign ; till at length the holy fpirit, feizing upon the faculties of fome one in the congregation, heats, agitates, and makes a prieft of him in an inftant. This infufion of the fpirit, is beftowed without exception of age, fex or condition. He who has been engaged all his life in the meaneft and moft infignificant occupations, and the circle of whofe ideas nature has circumfcribed within the moft narrow bounds, becomes all at once an oracle, and an interpreter of the fublime truths of chriftianity. The principal virtue of the Quakers ought to be *patience* ; for their *infpired* orators often put *it* to fevere proof, and the women, always attentive to the fuggeftions and dictates of this divine fpirit, make, it is faid, very free ufe of the precious gift of fpeech.

Such an extraordinary manner of worfhip, could not long retain its credit in the world, unlefs its followers manifefted greater fimplicity in their outward appearance, were more humane toward their fellow creatures, more upright in their dealings, and more difinterefted in civil fociety, than other men. But that enthufiafm, which firft gave birth to the fect, is now in a great meafure extinguifhed ; fo that we muft take them as they are in the prefent age, to form a proper opinion of them.

Such virtues as the above, in which the Quakers are faid to excel, have been more prevalent among them and of longer duration in America, than elfewhere, becaufe the climate and the life they lead is favourable thereto.

Piety, is not the only motive that brings the American Ladies in crowds to the various places of worfhip. Deprived of all fhows and public diverfions whatever, the church is the grand theatre where they attend, to difplay their extravagance and finery. There they come dreffed off in the fineft filks, and over-fhadowed with a profufion of the moft fuperb plumes. The hair of the head is raifed and fupported upon cufhions to an extravagant height, fomewhat refembling the manner in which the French ladies wore their hair fome years ago. Inftead of powdering, they often wafh the head, which anfwers the purpofe well enough, as their hair is commonly of an agreeable light colour ; but the more fafhionable among them begin now to adopt the pre-

fent

fent European method, of fetting off the head to the beft advantage. They are of a large fize, well proportioned, their features general-ly regular, and their complexion fair, without ruddinefs. They have lefs cheerfulnefs and eafe of behaviour, than the ladies of France, but more of greatnefs and dignity ; I have even imagined that I have feen fomething in them, that anfwers to the ideas of beauty we gain from thofe mafter-pieces of the artifts of antiquity, which are yet extant in our days. The ftature of the men is tall, and their carriage erect, but their make is rather flim, and their colour inclining to pale. They are not fo curious in their drefs as the women, but every thing upon them is neat and proper. At twenty-five years of age, the women begin to lofe the bloom and frefhnefs of youth; and at thirty-five or forty, their beauty is gone.

The decay of the men is equally premature, and I am in-clined to think that life itfelf is here proportionably fhort. I vi-fited all the burying grounds in Bofton, where it is ufual to infcribe upon the ftone over each grave, the names and ages of the deceafed, and found that few who had arrived to a ftate of manhood, ever ad-vanced beyond their fiftieth year ; fewer ftill to feventy, and be-yond that fcarcely any.*

Bofton is fituated on a peninfula, upon a defcent towards the fea fide ; this peninfula is connected with the continent only by a neck of land, which at full tide is not more than the breadth of a high way, fo that it would be no difficult matter to render this a place of great ftrength. Hard by is an eminence which commands the whole town, upon which the Boftonians have built a kind of light-Houfe or beacon, of a great height, with a barrel of tar fixed at the top, ready to fet fire to in cafe of an attack. At fuch a fig-nal, more than forty thoufand men would take arms, and be at the gates of the town in lefs than twenty-four hours.

From hence may be feen the ruins of Charleftown, which was burnt by the Englifh, on the 17th of June, 1775, at the battle of Bunker's Hill—a melancholy profpect, calculated to keep up in the breafts of the Boftonians, the fpirit and fentiments of liberty. This town was feparated from the peninfula only by *Charles* river, and was built in the angle formed by the junction of this river with the *Myftic*. The buildings in it were good, the whole ca-pable of being fortified to advantage, and feems to have been about half as big as Bofton.

The harbour of this laft mentioned city, can receive more than five hundred fail of veffels, but the entrance is difficult and dan-gerous, being only a channel about the breadth of three fhips. Some ftrong batteries, erected upon one of the adjacent iflands, protect the road, and confequently relieve the town from any ap-prehenfions of an infult from an enemy by fea. The capes that
bound

* *With the like attention, I examined all the church yards from Bofton to Williamfburg, almoft three hundred leagues, and found nearly the fame refult.*

bound the entrance of the bay,—the reef of rocks that edge the outlet of the road, and the little islands that are seen every where scattered up and down, form so many obstacles, which diminish and reprefs the sea-swell, and render this harbour one of the safest in the world.

The commerce of the Bostonians formerly comprized a variety of articles, and was very extensive before the breaking out of the present war. They supplied Great Britain with matts and yards for her royal navy, and built, either upon commission or their own account, a great number of merchantmen, remarkable for their superiority in sailing. Indeed they were of such a flight and peculiar construction that it did not require the abilities of a great connoisseur to distinguish their ships in the midst of those belonging to other nations. Those that they freighted on their own account were sent either to the American Islands or to Europe laden with timber, plank, joiners stuff, pitch, tar, tupentine, rosin, beef, falt pork and some furrs; but their principal object in trade was the codfish, which they caught upon their own coasts, and particularly in the bay of Maffachusetts. §

The product of this fishery was about fifty thousand quintals, annually, which they exported to the other neighbouring provinces, and even to Spain, Italy and throughout the Mediterranean, while those of the worst quality were destined to the use of the negroes in the Caribbee Islands. In this fishery they employed a great number of hands, and by this means furnished themselves with excellent failors. The province of Maffachusetts, tho' inferior to the rest in the quality of the soil, will always be rich and powerful while it retains this branch of commerce, and if at some future period this new world shall display a great and formidable force upon the sea, Boston will be the place from whence we shall first fee them advancing to affert an equal right to the watry Empire. In exchange for these exports they return with wine from Madeira, Malaga and Oporto, which they prefer to ours on account of their fweetnefs, or perhaps rather becaufe they are more accustomed to them.

From the Islands they bring vast quantities of sugar, which they confume with their *tea*, an article the North-Americans make use of at least twice a-day; molaffes they import in still greater quantities, they distil it into rum, which when mixed with water is their ordinary drink. The demand for this article was confiderable, and the quantity imported fo great that, before the war, it was not worth more than two shillings the gallon*. They often when in Europe, difpofed

§ *Cape Cod ftretches out into the fea in the form of a bent elbow, and forms a bay, having taken its name from this fifh. It is remarkable that the names here, like thofe of the ancients, are taken from the properties or fituation of the places, or the periods of their difcovery.*

* *The ſhilling in our money is worth 22 fols 6 Deniers, and the gallon is near four quarts of our meaſure.*

diſpoſed of their ſhips and cargoes together, and went over to England to purchaſe their manufactures, which they tranſported to America in Engliſh Bottoms, and thus the mother country increaſed, by the American commerce, the value of her own commodities, while ſhe ſupplied them only with articles of conſumption. By this double exchange with the Americans, the Engliſh manufactures were in great demand, although they could not be afforded ſo cheap as thoſe of other nations, owing to the exceſſive price of labour in England. Their fiſheries, their trade, and the vaſt number of veſſels they built has tendered them the carriers of all the Northern colonies.

It is computed that from 1748 to 1749, incluſive, there were 500 veſſels employed from this port in foreign commerce, and inward entries were made of 430; and the coaſting and fiſhing veſſels amounted to at leaſt 1000. It appears however that after this, as a certain Engliſh author remarks, their commerce had declined.

In 1738 forty-one ſhips were built at Boſton making in the whole 6380 tons; in 1743 were built 28; in 1746 twenty; in 1749 fifteen, amounting in all to 2450 tons. This decreaſe in the commerce of Boſton probably aroſe from ſeveral new eſtabliſhments that had been formed along the coaſt, which drew to themſelves thoſe different branches of trade which their ſeveral ſituations favoured them in.

The great demand for rum among the Americans led them to form connexions with the French Colonies: and our wines and brandies making this liquor of ſmall requeſt among us, they flattered themſelves that they could import molaſſes to advantage. This attempt ſucceeded beyond their expectations, although they had nothing to give in exchange but lumber, and ſome ſalt proviſions. But the Engliſh government perceiving the injury its own iſlands thereby ſuffered, prohibited this commerce entirely. The colonies, upon this, complained bitterly, and repreſented, that by hindering them from exporting the productions of their ſoil to what port they pleaſed, they would be rendered unable to pay for thoſe indiſpenſably neceſſary articles, which they purchaſed at an exorbitant price in England.

The government then took a middle way; permitted them the exportation of lumber, and loaded french ſugar and other foreign commodities imported, with very heavy duties. But this did not yet ſatisfy the colonies: they conſidered the mother country in the light of a jealous and avaricious ſtep-mother, watching every opportunity to turn to her own advantage thoſe channels of gain, which would have enabled them to live in eaſe and plenty. This was one of the principal cauſes of the miſunderſtanding between England and her colonies; from thenceforward the latter perceived what a change independence would make in their favour, and France was by no means ignorant of the political advantages that would accrue to her from ſuch a revolution.

The

The Irish Presbyterians, discontented with their landlords at home, and attracted by a similarity of sentiment, have established in this place, with some success, manufactories of linen, and have made some attempts at broad cloths; those that have been lately manufactured are close and well woven, but hard and coarse; their hat manufactories have succeeded not better than the cloths; they are thick, spungy and without firmness, and come far short of the beauty and solidity of ours.

The province of Massachusetts-Bay has mines of iron and copper; the iron is of a quality superior to any other in the world, and will bear hammering and drawing to a surprising degree.

The Europeans have long been convinced of the natural and moral dangers to be apprehended, in acquiring education in large towns. The Bostonians have advanced farther, they have prevented these dangers. Their University is at Cambridge, seven miles from Boston, on the banks of Charles River, in a beautiful and healthy situation. There are four colleges, all of brick, and of a regular form. The English troops made use of them as barracks in 1775, and forced the professors and students to turn out. The library contains more than 5000 volumes; and they have an excellent printing-house, well furnished, that was originally intended for a college for the native Indians. To give you an idea of the merit of the several professors it will be sufficient to say, that they correspond with the literati of Europe, and that Mr. Sewall, in particular, professor of the Oriental languages, is one of those to whom the author of genius and ability has been lavish of those gifts; their pupils often act tragedies, the subject of which is generally taken from their national events, such as the battle of Bunkers-Hill, the burning of Charlestown, the Death of General Montgomery, the capture of Burgoyne, the treason of Arnold, and the Fall of British Tyranny. You will easily conclude, that in such a new nation as this, these pieces must fall infinitely short of that perfection to which our European literary productions of this kind are wrought up; but still, they have a greater effect upon the mind than the best of ours would have among them, because those manners and customs are delineated, which are peculiar to themselves, and the events are such as interest them above all others: The drama is here reduced to its true and ancient origin. *

It

* *We confine our theatrical pieces either to fabulous heroes, the characters and manners of which have little or no resemblance to ours, and whose actions we can take no part in, or else araw our pictures of life from that class in society which are the least numerous, I mean the great and rich. The multitude can take no interest, can apply nothing to themselves in these performances, and must derive all their entertainment from some adventitious beauties, such as the connexion of the plan, the choice of the situations, the harmony of the verse &c. The Greeks, whom we have badly imitated, were in these points*
much

It is difficult to imagine what a strange idea the Americans had of the inhabitants of France, prior to the war; they looked upon them as a people bowed down beneath the yoke of despotism, given up to superstition, slavery, and prejudice, mere idolaters in their public worship, and, in short, a kind of light, nimble machines, deformed to the last degree, incapable of any thing solid or consistent ; entirely taken up with the dressing of their hair, and painting their faces ; without delicacy or fidelity, and paying no respect even to the most sacred obligations.—The English, it seems, were pleased to disseminate these prejudices amongst them, and confirm them therein; Presbyterianism, a most bitter enemy to the Catholic Faith, had likewise rendered the Bostonians, among whom this sect is predominant, more ready to listen to and believe them.

In the beginning of the war, every thing seemed to concur to strengthen these prejudices. The greater part of the French, who came into America at the first appearance of the revolution, were men loaded with debts, and ruined at home in their reputation ; and yet, by assuming titles and fictitious names, they obtained distinguishing ranks in the American army, received advances of money to a considerable amount, and then immediately disappeared. The simplicity of the Americans, added to their little experience, rendered these villanies less liable to be detected. Many of these adventurers even committed crimes in America, worthy of the most rigorous punishments.

The first commodities, too, that the Bostonians received from France, contributed, by their bad quality, to suggest unfavourable ideas respecting our upright dealing, and industry. For this reason, only, those goods which were imported hither from France, are

much more rational; all their dramatical subjects had a reference to their own mythology, form of worship, government, and the manners and customs of the several States; hence, their theatrical pieces could be supported without love fictions, or an absurd mixture of incidents. Much has been said about depravity of taste, perversion of manners, and so on, when the Parisians have been found to forsake the great theatres, and run to foreign exhibitions. But people deceive themselves in this matter ; those who flocked thither, with the greatest eagerness, were people most engaged in business, and consequently less corrupted in their manners than the great. Licentiousness was not their motive, but the pleasure of beholding the real scenes of life represented. Things interest us only so far as they resemble our own circumstances, and condition. The artist, who drew the picture representing the embarrassment and confusion of Paris, when about to leave the fair Helen, and the impetuosity of Hector reproaching him with his softness and effeminacy, forces me to admire his divine art in the handling of the subject, in the justness of the design, and in the life and harmony of the colouring : but Greuze, perhaps a less finished genius, and less regular, makes me tremble at the unnatural view of a father cursing his son, and does not even give me time to admire his beauties.

are fold at a confiderably lower price than Englifh articles, not in any refpeft fuperior.

At the arrival of the Count D'Eftaing, the people here were much furprifed to find that the French were not fuch weak, diminutive and deformed little mortals, as their prejudices had painted them : They however at laft concluded, that the Count and the people in his fleet, had been picked out on purpofe, in order to give them a more advantageous idea of the nation. Some coloured figures, having accidentally ftained one of the dreffing cloths, confirmed them in the opinion, that the French made ufe of vermillion to colour their faces.

Notwithftanding my being known for a Frenchman, and Roman Prieft, I was continually receiving new civilities from feveral of the beft families in this town ; but the people in general retain their old prejudices : I faw a remarkable proof of it one day from a trifling occurrence, which at the fame time ferved to give me a better idea of their character. The chimney of the houfe I lodged in, and which belonged to a Frenchman, happened to take fire : you may eafily conceive what an uproar this would occafion in a town chiefly conftructed of wood. The people collected in crowds ; but after they were told whofe houfe it was, they remained idle fpectators of the fcene. I then caufed the doors to be fhut to ftop the draft of air, and clofed up the chimney, in which the fire was, with a wet blanket ; we alfo threw water down inceffantly, to generate a moifture ; the women of the houfe, who were Americans, were however, much difpleafed at the fight of the floors, covered with water and foot ; and if we had not, in defpight of them, acted as we thought fit, I think they would rather have had the houfe burnt, than the floors and ceilings fpoiled.

We have juft heard the news of the capture of St. Euftatius by the Englifh : without doubt, avarice had a greater fhare in advifing this expedition, than found policy. The Americans, not pleafed with fuch of the French manufactures as were firft fent over, went thither to purchafe thofe of the Englifh, which after the war with Holland, were fent out to that ifland under neutral flags ; and thus they ruined one of their principal branches of commerce, and forced the Americans to have recourfe to our productions, which experience has now taught them to have a more favourable opinion of than before.

The arrival of the army, under M. le Comte de Rochambeau, at Rhode-Ifland, fpread a general terror through that place: the fields became mere deferts, and thofe whom curiofity led to vifit Newport * could fcarcely perceive a human form in the ftreet. Every

---

* This is the capital town of the State ; the goodnefs of its foil and the excellence of its climate have gained it the name of the Paradife of New-England : its trade was very flourifhing before the war : Befides its lumber and falt provifions, which were exported to the Iflands, they fent out large quantities of beer, cheefe, poultry and tallow.

Every Frenchman saw the absolute necessity there was for obliterating these prejudices, and every one sacrificed something to his own feelings, in order to accomplish this desired end. The superior officers established the strictest discipline among the troops; and the officers in general manifested upon every occasion that politeness and sweetness of behaviour peculiar to the nobility and gentry of France: In consequence of this the soldiery became mild, circumspect and moderate, and for a whole year there was not a single complaint made.

The French at Newport were no longer that fickle, presumptuous, blustering, haughty people that prejudice had pictured them; at the entertainments they gave, their whole behaviour was quiet and reserved, and their conversation confined to the American guests, to whom they became every day more and more dear. These young French noblemen, whom fortune, birth, and the habit of a court life, commonly leads to dissipation, luxury and a love of empty pomp, were the first to set the example of a simple and frugal manner of living; and they now shewed themselves as affable and as courteous to all, as if they had lived their whole lives with these citizens, in the quality of equals. This conduct, strictly persevered in, brought about a total change in the opinions of the Americans, regarding us. Even the Tories ‡ could not but respect the French, altho' they detested the cause they supported, and I am informed they were infinitely more affected with sorrow at the departure of the army, than they had been alarmed with fear at their arrival.

The French have in general, been upbraided a long time for paying no regard to the most sacred of all connexions, when their gallantry is concerned. Perhaps Newport may have afforded some examples. A French officer, by his attention and assiduity, gained the affections of a young and amiable lady. Her husband, who loved her tenderly, was soon convinced of the reality of this new attachment, and altho' afflicted in the most sensible manner, he did not discover his trouble to her either by complaints or reproaches; the reputation of his guilty spouse was still dear to him, and he was even afraid she would discover that he had knowledge of her infidelity. " And yet if she continues doubtful of it (said he to a friend) she will give over all hopes of regaining my esteem; her ruin will of consequence ensue, and my own peace be sacrificed: let us then endeavour to awaken her tenderness, and recall her to her duty by remorse for what is past." From this moment he became more assiduous and complaisant to her than ever; with sorrow and despair in his soul, he showed a countenance serene and satisfied. He received at his house, with attention and civility, the very officer who was the author of his misfortune; but, by the assistance of a friend, so contrived matters, as to hinder him from
any

‡ *Tories* i. e. *Royalists. This word is derived from the Saxon.*

any private interviews with her whatever. Thefe repeated difap-
pointments appeared to the Frenchman to be mere effects of chance;
he, however, grew fullen and peevifh upon it, and confequently
became lefs amiable in the eyes of the lady, and her hufband more
fo than ever; and thus, that virtue which had not loft all its claims
to her feduced heart, foon recalled it to its duty. Such a procedure
as this, in fo delicate an affair, difcovers great knowledge of the
human heart, and ftill more of dominion over itfelf.

The army left Newport the 9th of June to go, it is fuppofed, to
the Southward, and they are now actually at Providence. I am
juft fetting out to join it, and if it continues its march, I make no
doubt I fhall be enabled to entertain you with particulars ftill more
interefting.

LETTER II. *The author joins the French army at Providence.
Defcription of Providence.—Roger Williams, its founder.———
Fatigues of a military life.—Remarks on the drefs, fafhions and
food of the Americans.—Ignorance of the people of Connecticut in
point of making bread.—Their temper, peculiarities and character.
The foil and face of the country.—Hartford—the forefts and feveral
kinds of trees.—State of New-York.—Hudfon's river.—Devaftations occafioned by the War.*

SIR,
Camp, at Philipfburg, July 30, 1781.

I FOUND the army at Providence, encamped on a rifing ground.
This is a confiderable town, and pretty well peopled; fome of
the houfes are built of brick and others of wood; it is fituated at
the mouth of the river Patuxit, at the bottom of a bay betwixt the
States of Maffachufets, Connecticut, and Rhode-Ifland: This
fituation affords it a gainful commerce in corn, maize, lumber,
and falt provifions for the Iflands; there are alfo many veffels built
here.

This town is the capital of a colony of the fame name, Providence Plantation, now incorporated with the State of Rhode-Ifland.
A certain perfon, named Roger Williams, a minifter in Maffachu-
fetts-Bay, who had been banifhed by the magiftrates for preaching
up new doctrines, retired to this place with his followers, and
founded a colony, giving it the name of *Providence*, in order to
preferve to pofterity, the remembrance of the odious treatment he
had experienced. He there lived forty years in a rational folitude,
wholly taken up with improving this infant fettlement, and in-
ftructing the Indians; he alfo writ fome pieces againft the principles and practices of the Quakers, and, in the end, his regular
manner

manner of life, and benevolent conduct forced his enemies to repent of the infults they had offered him. And thus you fee, fir,
the annals of the new world furnish examples of an intolerant fpirit amongft a people, who have upon almoft every other occafion
fhowed themfelves the greateft enemies to it.

How different are the objects that now furround me, from thofe
which have hitherto taken up my time and attention ! Bred up in
the quiet retreats of the arts and fciences ; living conftantly with
thofe, who either cultivated or patronized them, and always defi-
rous to make them the companions of my labours and my pleafures—what a change do I experience now, when I am tranfported into the midft of the hurry of camps; all tumult and commotion
around me, and experiencing every moment a thoufand wants !
Here I am taught to fix the true value upon ufeful inventions, and
diftinguifh them from thofe which are only curious and whimfical.
A fingle fheet protects me from the inclemency of the weather ; and
being without books to divert my mind from the fatigues * I feel,
I frequently write, for want of ink, with the juice of an herb : happy, if I could reft for any length of time in tranquillity—but no
fuch thing—after two in the morning, the drum orders us univerfally out of our hard beds ; in hafte we roll up our travelling bed-
furniture, mount our horfes, and, with the flow pace of an Am-
baffador's train, follow the march of the foot-foldiers, bending
under the weight of the burden on their backs.

When, at length, arrived at the place deftined for our encampment, we have ftill to wait during the hotteft part of the day for
the baggage waggons, before we can take any repofe. The fun
has even fometimes almoft finifhed his courfe, before our weak
ftomachs have begun to receive and digeft the neceffary food:
ftretched at full length upon the ground, and panting with thirft,
I have often wifhed, like the rich man in the gofpel, that another
Lazarus would dip his finger in the water, to cool my parched
tongue. Our young Generals, who have been bred in eafe and
delicacy, bear up under thefe fatigues with a degree of refolution
that makes me blufh for my weaknefs. Whilft their tables, exhibiting at the fame time abundance and frugality, invite the officers to a ftile of living which the want of domeftics and other
neceffary means would render it impoffible for them otherwife to
enjoy, they encourage the foldiery under the feverity of duty by
marching before them on foot. § What you will moft wonder at, is,
that

* *The difficulty of providing a fufficiency of carriages, and finding
provifion to fupport the horfes or oxen, obliged Count Rochambeau to
order, that no officer fhould carry with him more than one hundred
and fifty pounds weight, including tents, beds, &c. and thus it happened in our long march, in a country where there are fo few refources,
that almoft all of us were in want of fome one neceffary or another.*

§ *M. le Vicomte de Noailles has in particular made a whole
campaign on foot.*

that the French never lose their cheerfulnefs and gaiety in thefe
painful and laborious marches. The Americans, whom curiofity
brings by thoufands to our camp, are conftantly received with
good humour and feftivity; and our military mufic, of which they
are extravagantly fond, is then played for their diverfion. At
fuch times officers, foldiers, Americans, of both fexes, all inter-
mingle and dance together;——it is the feaft of equality; and
thefe are the firft fruits of the alliance which is, we hope, to fubfift
perpetually between the two nations.

The fathers of the families melt at the fight of thefe affecting
fcenes; even thofe, who when they firft heard of our marc ing,
viewing us through the medium of prejudice and mifreprefenta-
tion, had trembled for their poffeffions, and for their lives. The †
foldier, inebriated with joy, forgets the fatigues of the morning,
nor makes himfelf wretched by anticipating thofe of to-morrow.
Thefe Americans being yet in that ftage of their national growth,
wherein the diftinctions of birth and rank are fcarcely known, confider the foldier and the officer in the fame point of view, and often
afk the latter, what his *trade* was in his own country ; not being
able to conceive, that the occupation of a foldier may be as fixed
and permanent as any trade whatever. The familiar appellation
of *brother*, given fome of them by the Marquis,* excited their curiofity and refpect to a great degree ; and the young American Ladies have always confidered it as one of their greateft honours, to
have danced with that nobleman.

Whatever may be the future fuccefs of this army, it will always
retain the glory of having made the moft lafting impreffions in thefe
countries, and rendered the memory of the French name dear and
precious to all ; an atchievement more flattering to true ambition,
and perhaps more difficult to accomplifh, than gaining battles, or
fpreading univerfal conqueft.

Before I arrived here, I had no expectations of difcovering the
traces of the French modes and fafhions, in the midft of the wilds
and forefts of America. The head dreffes of all the women,
except Quakers, are high, fpreading and decked profufely with our
gauzes: and here I cannot but reflect upon the oddnefs of their
tafte, when I find, through the whole ftate of Connecticut, fo
prevailing an inclination for drefs, (I may fay to a degree of extravagance) with manners at the fame time fo fimple and fo pure,
as to refemble thofe of the ancient patriarchal age. Pulfe, Indian
corn, and milk are their moft common kinds of food ; they alfo ufe
much *tea*, and this fober infufion conftitutes the chief pleafure of
their lives; there is not a fingle perfon to be found, who does not
drink

† *Their news-papers, during all our march, have never failed to
do juftice to the difcipline of our army.*

* *M. le Marquis de la Fayette is univerfally known to the
Americans, by his title of* Marquis.

drink it out of china cups and faucers, and, upon your entering a houfe, the greateft mark of civility and welcome they can fhow you, is to invite you to drink it with them. In countries where the inhabitants live upon foods and drinks of the moft fubftantial kind, it may be ufeful to the health, but I believe it is prejudicial in thofe where they fubfift moftly on vegetables and milk, efpecially when the foil, yet too much fhaded by the woods, makes them the lefs nourifhing; and perhaps this may be one of the caufes, that with a robuft and healthy conftitution, their lives here are much fhorter than thofe of the inhabitants of other countries. The lofs of their teeth is alfo attributed to the too frequent ufe of tea; the women, who are commonly very handfome, are often, at eighteen or twenty years of age, entirely deprived of this moft precious ornament; though, I am of opinion, this premature decay may be rather the effect of warm bread : for the Englifh, the Flemifh, and the Dutch, who are great tea drinkers, preferve their teeth found a long time.

The inhabitants of Connecticut, who raife fuch excellent corn, are, however, ignorant of the valuable art of rendering it more digeftive, and confequently more nourifhing, by thorough fermentation and kneading; whenever they want bread, they make a cake, which they fet to bake at the fire upon a thin iron plate. The French, whom the war brought into America, never could accuftom themfelves to this kind of bread, but did their endeavour to inftruct the natives how to bring it nearer to perfection : in the inns upon the road we found fome tolerably good, but far inferior even to that made in our army. The inhabitants who refide at a diftance from the high-ways preferve their ancient cuftoms in this and other particulars with great obftinacy, and believe no bread in the world to be better or more palatable than their own.

Scattered about among the forefts, the inhabitants have little intercourfe with each other, except when they go to church. Their dwelling-houfes are fpacious, proper, airy, and built of wood, and are at leaft one ftory in height, and herein they keep all their furniture and fubftance. In all of them that I have feen, I never failed to difcover traces of their active and inventive genius. They all know how to read, and the greateft part of them take the Gazette, printed in their village, which they often dignify with the name of town or city. I do not remember ever to have entered a fingle houfe, without feeing a huge family bible, out of which they read on evenings and Sundays to their houfhold. They are of a cold, flow and indolent difpofition, and averfe to labour; the foil, with a moderate tillage, fupplying them with confiderably more than they can confume: they go and return from their fields on horfeback, and in all this country you will fcarcely fee a traveller on foot: the mildnefs of their character is as much owing to climate as to their cuftoms and manners, for you find the fame foftnefs of difpofition even in the animals of the country. The horfes are of an excellent breed, and it is common for them to go

D long

long journeys at the rate of fifty or fixty miles a-day: they are very teachable, and it is a rare thing to find any of them ftubborn or fkittifh: the dog is here of a fawning, timid nature, and the ftrangeft figure of a man need not fear any violence from him. I have obferved, too, by the way, that his voice is rather broken and hoarfe, as well as that of the cock.

The Americans of thefe parts are very hofpitable ; they have commonly but one bed in the houfe, and the chafte fpoufe, altho' fhe were alone, would divide it with her gueft, without hefitation or fear. What hiftory relates of the virtues of the young Lacedemonian women, is far lefs extraordinary. There is here fuch a confidence in the public virtue that, from Bofton to Providence, I have often met young women travelling alone on horfeback; or in fmall riding chairs, through the woods, even when the day was far upon the decline.

In thefe fortunate retreats, the father of a family fees his happinefs and importance increafing, with the number of his children: he is not tormented with the ambitious defire of placing them in a rank of life, in which they might blufh to own him for a father. Bred up under his eye, and formed by his example, they will not cover his old age with fhame, nor bring thofe cares and vexations upon him, that would fink his grey hairs with forrow to the tomb. He no more fears this, than he would a fancied indigence, that might one day come upon him, wound his paternal feelings, and make the tender partner of his bed repent that fhe was ever the mother of children. Like him they will bound their cares, their pleafures, and even their ambition, to the fweet toils of a rural life, to the raifing and multiplying their herds, and the cultivating and enlarging their fields and their orchards.

Thefe American hufbandmen, more fimple in their manners than our peafants, have alfo lefs of their roughnefs, and rufticity ; more enlightened, they poffefs neither their low cunning nor diffimulation ; farther removed from luxurious arts, and lefs laborious, they are not fo much attached to ancient ufages, but are far more dexterous in inventing and perfecting whatever tends to the conveniency and comfort of life.

This country is interfected with an incredible number of rivers and rivulets; but Connecticut river is the moft confiderable in the whole State; the town of Hartford, fituate on its banks, is the capital, and confifts at prefent of not more than four or five hundred houfes, on a ftreet two miles in length. The river is deep enough to float veffels of about one hundred and fifty tons burthen, up to the town. The foil is light, except on the fouthern fide of the river, and yet it produces maize or Indian corn, and feveral other kinds of grain, in great abundance, the bread of which is much whiter than that in France, and the tafte equally excellent; this was a confiderable article of the American commerce with the iflands, where they neverthelefs preferred our European grain, being of a more mealy fubftance, and keeping fweet a much longer time.

time. The feveral kinds of wood here are much lighter than ours, and far lefs durable, as the roots are almoft at the furface of the ground: The foil being new, the vegetative particles are more abundant near the furface, and the roots, of confequence, direct themfelves horizontally, and thus they are more expofed to the impreffions of cold, heat, drought and moifture, and liable to be affected by the various changes of the atmofphere ; and, indeed, I have remarked, that the trees here almoft always begin to decay at the root.

I once imagined that thefe antique forefts, into which the arm of man had never carried the deftructive ftrokes of the ax, would have nothing to offer to the view, at every ftep, but ancient trees, whofe rugg-d, knotty, hollow trunks, were by rains and frofts, fupported nothing more than a dry naked top, ftripped of its extended boughs. Inftead of thefe venerable tokens of age that I looked for in the woodlands, I found every where the frefhnefs and vigour of youth the moft robuft. The trunks, clofe and compact, ftraight, and towering into the air beyond the reach of the eye, difplay from the top a multitude of branches, cloathed with a deeper green than ours can boaft of. The oak is by far the moft frequent to be met with ;—for the tree moft ufeful to man, is the tree of all climates ; and I have obferved no lefs than fix or feven different forts in this country : the leaves of one fort are broad with almoft imperceptible indentings, in others the incifions are ftill deeper, and in fome they are fo deep, that the principal fibres only remain extended ; a day or two ago I met with fome oaks, bearing leaves that are long and narrow and very much refembling thofe of the peach tree.

But the monarch of thefe forefts is the *tulip* or *yellow tree*; its afpiring top rifes above the loftieft oaks, and its thick extended branches project their fhadow to a very great diftance; its leaf compact, fmooth and flender, is fomewhat in fhape like a man's hand, with this difference, that the longeft fide appears to be cut tranfverfely. Each leaf is originally folded in a particular wrapper, formed fimply of two other leaves, of an oval fhape touching in every point of their circumference ; this principal leaf afterwards feparates the two others in order to expand and give room for growth, in the fame manner as a young bean fhoots out from between the leaves that confined it on each fide. The tulip, that brilliant flower, upon which our Florifts lavifh fuch a profufion of toil and expence, grows to the number of thoufands upon this ftately tree, refrefhes the eye of the American native, and perfumes the air which he breathes beneath its fhade. Out of this the Indians make their canoes or troughs, formed wholly of one piece; and in this particular the Englifh Americans have followed their example, making fome of them large enough to carry more than thirty men. Being of a nature fitted to flourifh in every climate, it would, I think, fucceed perfectly well in France ; more pleafant to the fight than the great chefnut tree, and more clean, it would

form

form woods and avenues full as thick and lofty, and its timber
would be infinitely preferable for every kind of joiner's work.
The faſſafras, an aromatic ſhrub, is found in open places, expoſed
to the ſun; alſo, on the ſides of the highways and along the ſkirts
of fields; its leaf reſembles that of the fig-tree, but not ſo large
nor ſo thick, and is of a paler green; it produces a ſmall fruit
growing in a pod, milky when it is green, and of a purple colour
when ripe; its odoriferous quality is reſident chiefly in the bark,
and particularly in that of the root; its property is ſudorific. Some
ſay, the firſt Europeans that came to America, being afflicted with
that dreadful *malady*, the progreſs of which has been ſo fatal in
Europe, made uſe of this ſhrub with ſucceſs.

We alſo found upon the banks of Connecticut river a ſort of
roſe-laurel, covered with flowers, and affording a delightful
proſpect to the eye. The gum-tree, which we found in low
interval lands, is a ſpecies of grove-laurel, the ſmell of which is
ſomewhat like that of our common laurel, but more agreeable; its
fruit, much like grains of pepper, is covered with an oily ſubſtance,
of which they make wax candles; the wax is drawn from the berry,
and collected by boiling them in water; and theſe candles when
burning emit a moſt delightful ſmell. But the proceſs is too
troubleſome, and the product too ſmall, for it ever to become an
object of commerce.

The maple-tree grows here to a very great ſize and is one of the
moſt valuable productions of all North-America: when the ſap
runsthey make inciſions in the body of the tree, from whence a rich
liquor flows out, which when boiled down, becomes a perfect
ſugar, and is uſed as ſuch. This tree perfectly reſembles our
maple in France, and yet why is it that it has this diſtinct property?
Can it be becauſe it vegetates in a new ſoil, where the juices are in
greater abundance for its nouriſhment, or rather are we yet ignorant
of the real properties of our maple? ‡

Cheſnut and walnut-trees are likewiſe very common here. The
laſt are various in their kinds, and the difference is known by the
leaf and the fruit: there is one ſort, the wood of which is full of
veins, and makes excellent turniture, and the outſide of its fruit
has conſiderably the ſmell of citron. They all produce nuts, the
kernel of which is not eaſy to come at, and they are beſides very
hard to break; the meat is not got out of the ſhell but with great
trouble, and by ſmall quantities, and after all the taſte is ſtrong
and diſagreeable.

We alſo found here a kind of bunch-cherry, ſmall and ſomewhat
bitter. The grape-vine, the culture of which they are wholly
ignorant

‡ *The author ſeems not to have known, that there are two ſorts*
of maple in America, very nearly alike in external appearance, but
of different properties. That here taken notice of is called the Sugar
maple, and grows in great quantities in the northern and weſtern parts
of New-York and Pennſylvania. TRANSLATOR.

ignorant of, even in Virginia, is seen every where climbing, and supporting itself upon the trees. *

It belongs to man to multiply, to fertilize and bring to perfection the useful productions of the various countries of the world,—by varying the soils, directing the course of the fap by pruning, and blending the several kinds of fruit, by means of ingrafting. We are indebted to the experience of many ages for thefe happy inventions, as well as for the ornaments and opulence of our gardens and orchards. Man, we may fay, is the reftorer of nature; he enlivens, enriches and beautifies it; the fimple turf that bedecks the ground, will only preferve its verdure in fuch places as he has expofed to the fun and air; the timid bird that flies from his fight, the wild beaft that trembles at his appproach, dwell only in thofe fequeftered haunts and folitary places which furround him at a remote diftance. If curiofi y has fometimes urged me to penetrate far into thefe gloomy forefts, I there no longer heard the voice, no longer traced the veftiges of animated beings, but walked only thro' pathlefs groves, and upon the faded ruins of the vegetable world. Saddening at this mournful filence, and the view of thofe lonely objects which difcovered no traces of the dominion of my own fpecies over the wild genius of nature, I haftened to revifit places and abodes, better calculated to enliven and gratify the foul of fenfibility.

The knowledge of the birds of this country will conftitute one of the moft interefting parts of its natural hiftory. I have feen in Connecticut a kind of ftarling, the middle part of whofe wings is of a deep red; and have obferved another bird of the colour of thofe brought from the Canary Iflands, but fomewhat larger. What they call the Virginian nightingale is more commonly met with as you advance to the South, but has no refemblance to ours ; it

* I have obferved two general forts of vines in America: the fruit of one of which was of a clofe contexture, plump, and as large as the fmaller fpecies of plumbs, but the tafte was intolerably infipid, and I do not believe that the culture of this fort would turn out to any advantage. The raifin, or flefhy part of the other, was fmall, the fkin hard and the kernel large, preferving a greenifh tafte even when ripe: I am convinced if this kind was cultivated with due care it would foon come to perfection. The vines we fee in France, in the vineyard provinces, growing at random in hedges without cutting or culture, are of a kind very little fuperior. The Englifh have tryed plantations of vines in Virginia, but never could fucceed. Inftead of bringing them from foreign countries, and cultivating them in the manner of thofe countries, they fhould have taken fuch as were natural to the foil, and given them a culture fuitable to the climate, and then fuccefs might be expected. The Roman catholic minifter at Baltimore, in Maryland, told me he had a vineyard of this fort, from which he had great expectations,

it is larger and its head and belly are of a red like that of the *Bouvreuil.* § If nature has been more bountiful to it in refpect of plumage, fhe has neverthelefs been far from granting it fo melodious a voice as ours. The mocking bird, almoft the fize of a thrufh, fpotted with white and grey, has the faculty of mimicking all other birds that it hears. The humming bird which they fay, lives only on the juice of flowers, is common enough, but, by the rapidity of its motions, there are few perfons that have ever had a diftinct view of it.

The fquirrels are of a pale afh grey, larger than ours, very common in the woods, and eafy to be tamed; thofe called flying fquirrels are of a darker grey, and fmaller in fize than the other; their fkin is large and loofe quite to the extremities of the paws, which they extend, when they leap from one branch of a tree to another, and thus are enabled to make ufe of a greater quantity of air, to fupport themfelves upon, as a bird does in flying.

The whole country, from Bofton to Providence, is level; and I have in this extent met with brooks, which we would call rivers; their beds, in thofe places where I paffed, looked as if they had been hollowed out of a foil of foft and fpungy ftone, of a grey and red complexion. I met, too, with fome blocks of petrified clay, inclofing pebbles or round flints, which, when ftruck upon, were eafily loofened, and left the mark of their form therein.

The whole State of Connecticut is covered with little hills, but the country is not fufficiently cleared of the wood, nor are they of fuch a fize, that we can eafily determine their general directions: for the moft part, we can only rank them in that clafs of hills which naturalifts denominate fecondary. They are often cut through, in order to render the defcent lefs fteep, and appear to me to be nothing but a mafs of ftones of different kinds and various fizes, with their corners broken and blunted. Many of them are more than a cubic foot in thicknefs, and fome three or four; the crevices between them being filled with a vegetable earth, that has little or no adherency to the ftone. The furface of the foil is covered with the fame kind of petrifactions, the woods and fields abound with them throughout, and to get rid of them the inhabitants of the country either throw them in heaps, or pile them up careleflly in form of a wall, on the lines that bound their poffeffions. Thefe ftones, from fome trials I have made upon them with *aqua fortis,* I find to confift of a gravelly, gritty fubftance, but not

subject

§ *This bird I take to be peculiar to the Eaftern continent. It is thus defcribed by a French writer.—" The Bouvreuil is a beautiful bird, very common in the foreft of Anet, and about the bignefs of a lark: the bill, head, wings and tail are black; the back a flate grey, and the belly of a beautiful red; it may be taught to talk and whiftle with very little trouble."* TRANSLATOR.

subject to diffolution by fire: Here is alfo the fpat ftone, (or ifinglafs) quite pure, and great plenty of talc; and others of thefe rocks abound with ferruginous particles, upon which the Load-ftone acts with confiderable effect.

The State of New-York, ftill more mountainous, and the territory of Philipfburg, where we are now encamped, prefents the fame objects to our view. So many millions of thefe ftones, lying in heaps, and fcattered through the fpace of more than two hundred miles, are the moft certain and authentic monuments of the long continuance of the waters on thefe countries. Torrents and rivers could never have thus rounded, intermixed and thrown them in heaps; the fea alone muft have feparated them by flow degrees, fcattered them into different parts, re-united, and impreffed on them thefe general forms by a continual attrition : But however attentively I have confidered things, I have not yet been able to find any veftiges of animal petrifactions, or of trees and fhells. The North-river has, in and about its bed, very few ftones of the granite kind, but plenty of marble, free-ftone and flate.

As we approach towards New-York, between the Lines of both Armies, we fee more and more of the forrowful veftiges of war and defolation,—the houfes plundered, ruined, abandoned or burnt. Thefe Americans fo foft, pacific and benevolent by nature, are here transformed into monfters implacable, bloody and ravenous; party rage has kindled a fpirit of hatred between them; they attack and rob each other by turns, deftroy dwelling houfes, or eftablifh themfelves therein by driving out thofe who had before difpoffeffed others.* War, that terrible fcourge to arts and population, is ftill more fo to the morals of a people, becaufe a change in thefe for the worfe is more difficult to repair.   I am &c.——

* Some of them, lying in ambufcade fired upon two of our Aids de camp and upon M. Berthier, as they were going to make fome obfervations upon New-York. They were, however, purfued, one taken, and M. Berthier killed another with his own hand. To this gentleman and his brother we are indebted for an exact map of the country, containing the whole rout of the French army from Newport to York in Virginia.

LETTER

LETTER III. *Junction of the French and American armies
at Philipsburg.—West-Point.— Expedition of a party of English to
Tarry-Town.— Bravery of thirteen French soldiers.— A detachment of French and Americans, march to reconnoitre the works at
New-York.— General Washington.— Remarks upon the American
army.—Their military dress, and manner of living —Discipline.—
Uncertainty of the object of the Campaign.—Various opinions.—
Improbability of succeeding in an attack upon New-York. —Marquis
de la Fayette, and his army in Virginia.—A march to the Southward not unlikely.*

Camp, at Philipsburg, August 4, 1781.

THE chief object of our marching, was to form a junction with
the army of General Washington : this junction was effected at Philipsburg. The Americans arrived there about the same
time we did, having been before entrenched upon the mountains
of West-Point, that command the North-River. The stream being very narrow in this part, the Americans have built forts upon
each side, the batteries of which traverse each other. The fort upon the left side, is situated upon a slip of land that runs out into the
river, covered on the east by a marsh, and only open on the
north. An army is there in a situation to repel an attack from a
far superior force, and the batteries of the forts can prevent any
vessel whatever from sailing farther up: This situation is the more
important to the Americans, as the English are at present masters
of New-York, and consequently command the entrance of the
North-River.

As allies, we are encamped to the left of the Americans, and
their right is extended upon the North-River, as low as Dobbs'
ferry : our left is upon a little river called the Bronx. The position of both armies is upon considerable heights, and a deep valley
separates us. We are not more than fifteen miles from New York,
but to get there, we should be under the necessity of marching down
the whole length of the island, and traversing a country full of
armed refugees. The French army, ever since it began its march,
had been parcelled out into distinct regiments, but upon our
approach to New-York, it was re-united into a brigade. Being
now necessitated to march in a single column, and having our
baggage waggons drawn by oxen, our progress was proportionably
slow and confused, the whole body, occupying an extent of several
miles. We had also to fear, least, in these mountainous and woody
regions parties of the enemy might come and fall upon our baggage and artillery, burn them, and hamstring the oxen and horses,
before we could have it in our power to relieve them. These losses,

in

in our situation, would have been irreparable; the English, how-ever, although greatly interested in preventing our joining the Americans, never made the least movement to hinder it.

A march of two hundred and fifteen miles through the most excessive heats, in a country very defective in supplies for an army, where the soldier is often in want of bread, and is obliged to carry provisions for several days with him, has neverthelefs made fewer invalids among us, than if we had laid still in a garrison. It is true, the strict attention of the superior officers has greatly contri-buted thereto, in never suffering the men to drink water, except with a quantity of rum intermixed, to take away its injurious qua-lities. M. le Comte Saint-Maime, Colonel commandant de Soiffonnais, always at each halt, and each place of encamping, fent out, and purchafed barrels of cider, which he caufed to be diftributed among his troops, at a very low rate. His example was afterwards followed by the other corps, and produced the happieft effects.

The English, fince our encamping with the Americans, having laid a plan to intercept the fupplies we received from the back country by means of the North-River, fent up a twenty gun frigate, and fome floops as far as Tarry-town, a village fituated fix miles upon the right flank of the rear of the army. Two hun-dred men made an attempt to land, and the firft company that difembarked had time to fet fire to fome great gun carriages, to a batteau, and to take off another loaded with fix thoufand rations of bread; but a fergeant of the regiment of Soiffonnais, and twelve foldiers, forced them to re-embark, and even entered waift deep into the water to purfue them, and hindered the reft from coming on fhore. This firft feat of the French arms in America gave the English fome idea of what they were to expect from the united efforts of a whole corps. The commanding officers ftrove who fhould be foremoft in beftowing praifes upon thefe brave foldiers: " My general (anfwered the fergeant to M. le Baron de Viomenil, who was extolling his bravery to the fkies) I am indebted to the good advice and bravery of my corporal for what I have done, for he perfectly feconded my endeavours." Courage is not a rare virtue in France, but modefty is fomewhat more fo, and yet this was a pattern of the moft perfect modefty, in a circumftance very delicate for a foldier. I have, I affure you, heard with pain a fuperior officer find fault with the encomiums that were given thefe men, and blame M. le Baron de Viomenil for having afterwards invited them to dine with him.——Can virtue ever be too much honoured, or too well rewarded?

Batteries were erected in hafte, as low as Dobbs's ferry, and when the English frigate and floops came down, they had to fuftain a very heavy cannonade: a fhell from a mortar piece fet the frigates fails on fire, and terror and confufion feemed pre-dominant among the crew, twenty-two of whom threw themfelves overboard into the river, and were moftly drowned.

E   General

General Wafhington, having fignified his intentions of reconnoitring the fortifications of New-York; two thoufand French,
and as many Americans, fet out on their march to efcort him,
and, at break of day, found themfelves within cannon fhot of the
enemy's intrenchments: they remained there two days, while the
Englifh contented themfelves with now and then firing a cannon,
and obferving their motions at a diftance.

I have feen General WASHINGTON, that moft fingular man—
the foul and the fupport of one of the greateft Revolutions that has
ever happened, or can happen again. I fixed my eyes upon him
with that keen attention, which the fight of a great man always
infpires—We naturally entertain a fecret hope of difcovering in the
features of fuch illuftrious men, fome traces of that excellent genius
which diftinguifhes them from, and elevates them above their fellow mortals. Perhaps the exterior of no man was ever better calculated to gratify thefe expectations, than that of General Wafhington : He is of a tall and noble ftature, well proportioned, a
fine, chearful, open countenance, a fimple and modeft carriage ;
and his whole mien has fomething in it, that interefts the French,
the Americans, and even enemies themfelves, in his favour. Placed
in a military view, at the head of a nation, where each individual
has a fhare in the fupreme legiflative authority, and where the co-
ercive laws are yet in a great degree deftitute of vigour, where the
climate and manners can add but little to their energy, where the
fpirit of party, private intereft, flownefs, and national indolence
flacken, fufpend and overthrow the beft concerted meafures ;
although fo fituated, he has found out a method of keeping his
troops in the moft abfolute fubordination : making them rivals in
praifing him ; fearing him even when he is filent, and retaining
their full confidence in him, after defeats and difgrace.—His re-
putati n has at length arifen to a moft brilliant pitch ; and he may
now grafp at the moft unbounded power, without provoking envy,
or exciting fufpicions. He has ever fhown himfelf fuperior to fortune, and in the moft trying adverfity has difcovered refources till
then unknown ; and as if his abilities only increafed and dilated
at the profpect of difficulty, he is never better fupplied than when
he feems deftitute of every thing ; nor have his arms ever been fo
fatal to his enemies, as at the very inftant when they thought they
had crufhed him forever.—It is his to excite a fpirit of heroifm
and enthufiafm in a people, who are by nature very little fufcep-
tible of it ; to gain over the refpect and homage of thofe whofe intereft it is to refufe it, and to execute his plans and projects by
means unknown even to thofe who are the inftruments ; he is in-
trepid in dangers, yet never feeks them but when the good of his
country demands it, preferring rather to temporize and act upon
the defenfive, becaufe he knows fuch a mode of conduct beft fuits
the genius and circumftances of his nation, and that all he and
they have to expect, depends upon time, fortitude, and patience :
he is frugal and fober in regard to himfelf, but profufe in the public

lic caufe ;—like Peter the Great, he has by defeats conducted his army to victory ; and like Fabius, but with fewer refources and more difficulty, he has conquered without fighting, and faved his country.

Such are the ideas that arife in the mind, at the fight of this great man, in examining the events in which he has had a fhare, or in liftening to thofe whofe duty obliges them to be near his perfon, and confequently can beft difplay his true character.——In all thefe extenfive ftates, they confider him in the light of a beneficent God, difpenfing peace and happinefs around him—Old men, women and children, prefs about him when he accidentally paffes along, and think themfelves happy, once in their lives, to have feen him—they follow him through the towns with torches, and celebrate his arrival by public illuminations.——The Americans, that cool and fedate people, who in the midft of their moft trying difficulties, have attended only to the directions and impulfes of plain method and common reafon, are roufed, animated and inflamed at the very mention ot his name ; and the firft fongs that fentiment or gratitude has dictated, have been to celebrate General Wafhington.

It is uncertain how many men his army confifts of exactly : fome fay, only four or five thoufand, but this General has always found means to conceal the real number, even from thofe who compofe it. Sometimes with a few troops he forms a fpacious camp, and increafes the number of tents ; at other times with a great number, he contracts it to a narrow compafs ; then again by detaching them infenfibly, the whole camp is nothing more than the mere fkeleton and fhadow of an army, while the main body is tranfported to a diftant part of the country.

Neither do thefe troops in general wear regular uniforms ; but the officers and corps of artillery are obliged, without exception, to fuch diftinction. Several regiments have fmall white frocks, with fringes, which look well enough ; alfo linen over-alls, large and full, which are very convenient in hot weather, and do not at all hinder the free ufe of the limbs in marching : with food lefs fubftantial, and a conftitution of body lefs vigorous than our people, they are better able to fupport fatigue, and perhaps for that very reafon. This advantage in drefs, I believe, has not been fufficiently confidered in France. We are apt to confult the gratification of the eye too far, and forget that troops were defigned to act, and not merely to fhow themfelves and their finery. The moft proper apparel would be that, which being as little burdenfome as poffible, would cover the foldier beft, and incommode him the leaft. The regiment of Soiffonnais has in all this tedious march, had the feweft ftragglers and fick of any other ;—one of the principal caufes was, without doubt, the precaution of the Colonel, who, on purpofe for the campaign, had linen breeches made for his whole regiment.

The

The American military habit, altho' eafy to be foiled, is never-thelefs very decent and neat; this neatnefs is particularly obfervable among the officers; to fee them, you would fuppofe they were equipped with every neceffary in the completeft manner, and yet upon entering their tents, where perhaps three or four refide together, I have often been aftonifhed to find, that their whole travelling equipage and furniture would not weigh forty pounds; few or none have matraffes; a fingle rug or blanket, ftretched out upon the rough bark of a tree, ferves them for a bed; the foldiers take the fame precaution never to fleep on the ground, whilft ours prefer it to any other way.

Their manner of living is very fimple, and gives them but little trouble; they content themfelves with broiling their meat, and parching their corn, or baking unleavened dough, made of Indian meal, upon the hot embers.

In fome regiments they have negro companies, but always commanded by the whites.

Their difcipline is exceeding fevere, and the power of the officers over the foldiers is almoft unlimited, lafhing them with whips, and beating them with canes for the flighteft faults: I, with fome French officers, was accidentally a witnefs to their rigorous mode of chaftifement; the criminal was tied to the wheels of a cannon carriage, his fhoulders naked, his arms ftretched out, in order to give the mufcles their greateft tenfion, and in this fituation every foldier of the company came up and gave him a certain number of ftrokes, with a large whip, which foon covered him with blood; what aftonifhed us moft, and detained us the longer at this difagreeable fpectacle, was, that two of thefe unhappy culprits, who both fuffered the fame degree of punifhment, never uttered the leaft groan or complaint, or fhowed any figns of fear. Is this courage, or is the natural fenfibility of mankind lefs acute among a people, where the air of the forefts and the conftant ufage of tea and milk, foften and relax the fibres to a moft aftonifhing degree?

Notwithftanding the actual appearance of our Generals before New-York, the object of the prefent campaign remains very uncertain: fome fay the Americans are tired of the war, and difcontented with our inactivity, and for that reafon the French army has joined them, folely to re-animate their drooping courage. It is alfo reported, that fince the defection of Arnold, General Wafhington, not altogether fatisfied with the fidelity of his army, has come to a refolution of trufting the important poft of Weft-Point to the French. The views of this general, in my opinion, extend farther than all this. We have juft learnt that *M. de Barras*, commander of our fquadron at Rhode-Ifland, has received fome tidings of *M. de Graffe*, and has fent him a frigate, with a number of pilots on board for thefe coafts. This looks as if New-York was their object. That Ifland and city is, at prefent, the general ftore houfe of the Englifh, and the centre of their operations; the

poffeffion

poffeffion of this place enables them to hold an eafy communication with their territories to the north and fouth, and at the fame time to menace the interior parts of the adjacent country by means of Hudfon's river, and prevent the forces of the North-Eaftern States from advancing to the Southward: it is alfo a fecure receptacle for their fleets, where they can plan and prepare for their offenfive operations, in the Weft India Iflands. The capture of this place would be a decifive ftroke; and from the moment fuch an event takes place, the Englifh muft forever renounce the hope of fub-jecting the States; and in their prefent exhaufted fituation, I do not fee how they would even repair the lofs of the ftores and the troops.—Charleftown and Savannah, having to oppofe the whole impreffion and ftrength of the American continental forces, would make but a poor defence, and the Iflands, ftill more difficult to be relieved by timely affiftance, would lie entirely at the mercy of an enemy.

On the other hand, New-York is well fortified and defended, both by land and water, and the fortifications very extenfive; it is, befides, garrifoned by the beft troops of Great Britain, amounting to fifteen thoufand men, including the troops raifed in the country; fo that to lay fiege to New-York there would be wanting, befides a fuperior maritime force, at leaft thirty thoufand men; whereas, our combined army does not amount to much more than ten thoufand; it is true the militia of the country may be collected, but thefe are nothing more than undifciplined troops, the duration of whofe fervice is always limited; and what could fuch do againft regular forces, well intrenched, and inured to all the dangers and hardfhips of war, for fix or feven campaigns? Even the French army, however brave and well difciplined it may be, is compofed of troops, very few of whom have ever been actually in a battle. At any rate, a fiege of this place would be long and tedious, and as to the fquadron of M. de Graffe, we know it cannot leave the Weft-India Iflands till the Hurricane feafon comes on, and can only remain here during that feafon, otherwife his projected operations in thofe feas would fail, and our poffeffions lie expofed to the enemy.

If, on the other hand, this important expedition fhould fail, all would be ruined: the Americans exhaufted, and difcouraged at the revolt of Arnold, panting after repofe, and viewing us in the light of a feeble Ally, would lofe courage, turn their views towards peace, and perhaps purchafe it at any price whatever.

The South is, moft probably, the real object of this campaign: Thofe States have for a long time felt all the miferies of war, and have been wafted alternately by friends and enemies. Virginia has been the fcene of the cruelties and devaftations of Arnold; and Cornwallis, difquieted at the news of our marching, has quitted Charleftown and traverfed, with a large body of troops, the Caro-linas and Virginia; at the fame time plundering the fettlements, kidnapping

kidnapping the negroes, and spreading death and desolation wherever he happened to march. So many repeated distresses and losses have discouraged the inhabitants, and inclined them to do any thing at all to better their situation. The arrival of our army among them, can alone free them from oppression, and revive their courage.

A certain *warrior*, [*Marquis de la Fayette*] at the head of twelve or fifteen hundred men, has nevertheless found means to keep his ground all this time in Virginia ; the impetuous Arnold, and the active Cornwallis, not daring to attempt any thing against him. You will doubtless suppose, that this *warrior* is one of those men, whom long experience and brilliant successes, have rendered formidable to the enemy. This leader, I assure you, is a man of only twenty-four years of age, who has left the arms of an affectionate and amiable wife, a residence among pleasures and high life, where his name, and an alliance with an illustrious family, opened a way to the greatest dignities, to come to this country, and, under the American FABIUS, defend the sacred cause of liberty, and learn to serve his king and country. The word *Marquis*, which has been so long used among us, to characterize foppish ficklenefs and levity, universally excites admiration and gratitude, at the very mention of of it, throughout the American world.

A southern expedition would be less hazardous in its nature, and less decisive in its effects, than here, but more pressing upon the enemy, and promising a more certain prospect of success. We have intelligence, that Lord Cornwallis is fortifying at York, a small town in Virginia, situated upon a river of the same name. This news begins to elevate the spirits of the French, who, if they could once hear of the arrival of M de Graffe, would conclude, that this campaign would not yet go over without some considerable events.

Several of our officers employed their leisure time last winter, in making a tour to the southward. One of them, M. de Saint Victor, Captain in the regiment of Soiffonnais, and well known to be very skillful in every particular that regards his profession as a soldier, and who did not make this tour without reaping considerable advantage from it, has viewed *York*, and judges it incapable of being fortified to any great purpose, being destitute of an opening for a retreat; so that having a squadron that could command Chefapeak-Bay, in his opinion, we could soon bring the enemy to what terms we pleased.

It is difficult, however, to persuade one's self, that Cornwallis, who knows the country so well, and has acquired so much reputation in this war, and who is by no means ignorant of the motions of our armies, would pitch upon such a situation, without he was convinced it would every way answer his purposes. An enemy is oftentimes never more to be dreaded, than when he appears to give you advantages over him.——The season being pretty well advanced

vanced, we cannot remain much longer in a state of uncertainty. In my next letter, I hope I shall be able to give you an account of matters with a greater degree of precision.

I am, &c.

LETTER IV. *New-York menaced by the Allied Army on the side of King's-bridge and Staten-Island.—The possession of this island absolutely necessary, before any attempt can be made upon Long-Island or New-York.—Ardour of the troops for action.*

Camp at Philipsburg August 15. 1781.

GENERAL Washington and Count Rochambeau passed the North-River a few days ago, and have ever since been reconnoitring. They who supposed we were to direct our rout towards Virginia, begin now to think they were deceived: part of the army, on this side, are preparing to march down by the way of King's-bridge; and on the other side, orders are given to get ready to proceed towards Staten-Island, and even to construct ovens to bake bread for the troops, when arrived in that quarter; others again are ordered towards Philadelphia.—What are we to think? All this seems to me like our theatrical marches, where the concern and perplexity of the spectators is continually increasing; I am in doubt, whether the unravelling of the matter will compenfate for the trouble, anxiety, and uneasiness it occasions.

Staten-Island, they say, is garrisoned by eight or nine hundred regular forces, so that the capture of it would be a most brilliant affair: It is separated from Long-Island only by a streight of two or three miles over, and our being such near neighbours, would perplex the English greatly, and put us in a situation to attempt something upon the larger island, with a better prospect of success. Our troops are full of ardour and confidence, and the several commanders seem calculated by nature to inspire them with a spirit of boldness and enterprize. General Washington, in particular, animates them by his presence, by the idea they have of his military talents; by his local knowledge of the country, and by that impenetrable veil of secrecy, under which he revolves and matures all his great designs. It is said the army will move in a day or two, which will enable us to determine the better to what quarter we are to proceed.

I am, &c.

LETTER

LETTER V. *The main body of the army returns to North-Castle.—The author lost in the woods, and in great danger from the Refugees —The combined forces march into the Jerseys.—Staten-Island threatened with a descent.—Surprising inactivity of the English, at New-York.—An expedition to Virginia, the real object of the army.—General view of New-Jersey—Character of the people.—The army arrives at Princeton.*

Princeton, September 1, 1781.

AT length, Sir, I can inform you that the army left Philipsburg the 19th. of last month, and having made a retrograde movement, returned to *North Castle*, twenty-two miles distant. A heavy rain rendered this march very disagreeable, for instead of reaching that place at ten or eleven in the morning, as we expected, we did not arrive till eight o'clock the next day; both officers and soldiers having spent the night in the roads in the most dismal weather, and water half leg deep. Neither was I exempt from the general misfortune; for I had imprudently advanced, unaccompanied, some miles before the army, and got into a road infested with Refugees (who never grant quarter to Frenchmen) where a domestic of mine escaped from them very narrowly, and had he not been armed, would doubtless have lost his life. They have lately hanged a Secretary belonging to one of our Commissaries, and assassinated an officer of the legion of Lauzun; so that I will confess to you, when I found myself alone and defenceless in these woods, I was in dread of adding to the number of those who have fallen victims to the resentment of these enemies of republicanism; yet I had the good fortune to arrive safe at the camp, having passed the night without tent or shelter of any sort, stretched out by a large fire, roasting on one side, and half drowned on the other,— and even found means to sleep several hours. How many of you rich sluggards, under your gilt cielings, and upon your beds of down, have not been able to do as much!

The inhabitants of the country were greatly surprised to see us returning the same road so soon, and the *tories*, with a malicious sneer, demanded *if we were going to rest from our labours:* but it was not long before they discovered the feint.

We were now advanced considerably up the North-river, and in three days were as high as King's ferry, but the Americans, having travelled along the river side, had arrived there before us.

Some have alledged, that if the English had sent some armed vessels up the Hudson, they might have retarded us considerably, and done us infinite mischief. The retrograde march that we made by order of General Washington, was doubtless meant to divert
them

them from this attempt; but neverthelefs, after the trial they had of the abilities of our artillery men, they muft have known they would run a great rifque of having their veffels deftroyed efpecially if they had met with calms or contrary winds.

The allied army has croffed a great part of the State of New-Jerfey, drawing a large quantity of batteaus with them upon carriages, and always menacing Staten-Ifland. It proceeds in two columns, the Americans forming that next to the fea, although their number does not exceed five or fix thoufand. The inactivity of the Englifh, at this critical moment, is really incomprehenfible; they might, without rifquing a great deal, harrafs our army, and do us irreparable mifchief, and they have all the reafon in the world to make fuch an attempt, for altho' General Wafhington has had the dexterity to keep them in uncertainty hitherto, they cannot be ignorant that we are in hourly expectations of the arrival of Count de Graffe upon thefe coafts; and they know that Admiral de Barras has embarked all his heavy cannon, and made prepara-tions for failing. It is their intereft to prevent the junction of our forces, and what more favourable opportunity could there be, than when the army was marching through a country covered with fteep mountains, thickfet with woods, and interfected with rivers, and where for want of fupplies, the troops muft march in a lefs compact ftate than they would otherwife do.

There is now fcarcely any doubt but that we are going to Virginia, unlefs we fuppofe the immediate arrival of Count de Graffe fhould oblige the army to return northwards.

This part of the country is wholly different from that we have hitherto traverfed: it is not, like Connecticut, covered with fmall hills lying clofe together, which render travelling difficult, obftruct the view, and prevent one from forming a clear idea of the whole fcene. Many ridges of mountains, which feem to be branches of the Apalachian, ftretch from north eaft to fouth weft, and form intervals of vaft and beautiful plains, which the hand of the geometrician feems to have fmoothed to a level. Thefe plains are adorned with large and handfome edifices; and the country abounds with orchards, fields of wheat, rye, barley, indian corn, and flourifhing woods.—The inhabitants, for the moft part of Alfacian and Dutch defcent, are gay, eafy and engaging in their manners, and refemble the happy region they inhabit. Provifions are brought into our camp from all quarters; and thofe that bring them are commonly wealthy people, and very unlike our traders in fruits and pulfe. You will often fee the women decked with their head dreffes and gauzes, riding in their farm waggons to market, drawn by the moft elegant horfes.

I have taken the pains to travel over the fummits of thefe high mountains of Jerfey, and find them to confift principally of rocks of granite, of different kinds, adhering very clofe together, but aqua fortis, when applied thereto, produces no ebullition: ifin-glafs is found here likewife in the greateft abundance. If thefe

F   mountains,

mountains, which muſt neceſſarily be ranked in the primitive claſs, owe their origin to a vitrified matter, which had once been in a ſtate of fuſion for ſeveral thouſand years, they would neceſſarily be homogeneous; but I do not remember that I ever found here a mixture of ſeveral ſubſtances, re-united in grains, aſſuming regular forms and different colours. Be that as it will, theſe mountains muſt have undergone great revolutions, for they are ſplit aſunder in many places, and fragments of a prodigious bulk are removed a conſiderable diſtance from their firſt ſituation: upon one of the loftieſt of theſe hills, I met with a monſtrous block of ſtone, ſtanding by itſelf, rounded at its angles, ſupported upon a very ſmall baſis, and apparently upon the point of tumbling down, and rolling away—what was its original poſition, or who could have raiſed it to this height?

The village of Princeton is inconſiderable, but remarkable for its charming ſituation, elegant houſes, and above all, a college built of ſtone, four ſtories high, having twenty-five windows in the front, in each ſtory. In the college, I ſaw two grand performances of mechaniſm; one of which repreſents the motions of the heavenly bodies, according to the ſyſtem of Newton and Copernicus.* The inventor of it is an American, and reſides at Philadelphia.—I have been aſſured, that he is now making another, exactly ſimilar, to preſent to that auguſt *Monarch*, whoſe alliance and Friendſhip ought forever to excite ſentiments of gratitude in the minds of theſe weſtern people.   I am, &c.

LETTER VI. *Trenton—The beauty of its ſituation.—River Delaware.—The capture of the Heſſians, in 1776.*

Trenton, September 2, 1781.

WE were yeſterday encamped in the vicinity of a very agreeable little town; and although we are to day but twelve miles from it, we are come in view of another not at all inferior to it, in pleaſantneſs and the ſalubrity of the air, and ſituated to much better advantage: It is the largeſt we have ſeen ſince our leaving Providence, and ſtands upon the north eaſtern bank of the Delaware, twenty-ſeven miles above Philadelphia. This advantageous ſituation, makes it a place of conſiderable trade, and intercourſe with the capital of Pennſylvania, eſpecially in the article of proviſions. The Delaware is navigable thus far up, for veſſels of ſome tolerable burden, but afterwards becomes all at once ſo ſhallow, that a little above the town carriages may paſs ſafely over at the fording places, when the tide is out. The ſhores of this river have nothing of that gloomy and ſavage aſpect obſervable on the Hudſon; they are, on the contrary, as level and pleaſant as thoſe of the Loire. The ſoil is light here, as well as in moſt other places we have ſeen, but at the ſame time very excellent. The maize, or

Indian

This is the famous Orrery by Rittenhouſe.

Indian corn, a plant that infinitely exhausts the ground, grows luxuriant here, even in those lands which have been cultivated for a century past, and is in height from seven to eight feet ; the stalks are plump and vigorous, and the ears long and heavy.

General Washington has rendered this place famous to the latest times, by a victory, in which he so happily disclosed the amazing resources of his genius.

The English troops in 1776, being arranged in cantonments, formed a line from Brunswick, on the river Raritan, to the Delaware; fourteen or fifteen hundred men were at Trenton, as many at Bordentown, and a third corps of equal strength at Burlington, which is only twenty miles from Philadelphia. General Washington's army, which had scarcely dared to show itself the whole campaign, and was every day growing weaker and weaker, left the English in enjoyment of the greatest security, and only two nights freezing weather would have enabled them to cross the Delaware on the ice, and take possession of Philadelphia. In this critical situation of affairs the *Congress* retired to Baltimore in Maryland, and America, with dread and consternation, beheld the fatal moment approaching, when her chains were to be rivetted on her forever.

General Washington, not finding himself in a situation to make head against the united force of the enemy, formed a design of attacking them separately : In haste he collected the militia of Pennsylvania, Maryland, and Virginia, and divided the whole into three bodies; two could not pass the Delaware for the ice, but that party under the direction of the General himself was more fortunate ; for he crossed the river, and after a smart conflict, took above nine hundred Hessians prisoners. A short time afterwards, having kindled fires through his camp, and left one man to take care of each, he marched round about, and came upon the rear of the enemy, surprised them once more, near Princeton, and obliged another considerable body to surrender their arms. The English were then, in their turn, forced to retire, and put themselves on the defensive.

To-morrow we pass the Delaware, and in two days more shall have a sight of the residence of the American Congress; I shall forget nothing that may appear to me deserving of your attention,

I am, &c.

LETTER

LETTER VII. *The French army reach Philadelphia.*——
Encamp on a plain near the Schuylkill.— *Review of the Regiment of*
Soiſſonnais —*Firſt intelligence of the arrival of Count de Graſſe in*
the Cheſapeke.—*Charles Thomſon.*— *Deſcription of Philadelphia.*—
The ſeveral religious ſeɛts there.——*Continental Congreſs.*——
State-Houſe.—*Philoſophical Society.*

Philadelphia, September, 6, 1781.

THE arrival of the French army at Philadelphia was more
like a triumph, than ſimply a paſſing through the place:
the troops made a halt about a quarter of a league from the city,
and in an inſtant were dreſſed as elegantly as ever the ſoldiers of a
garriſon were upon a day of review: they then marched through
the town, with the military muſic playing before them, which is
always particularly pleaſing to the Americans; the ſtreets were
crowded with people, and the ladies appeared at the windows in
their moſt brilliant attire. All Philadelphia was aſtoniſhed to ſee
people, who had endured the fatigues of a long journey, ſo ruddy
and handſome, and even wondered that there could poſſibly be
Frenchmen of ſo genteel an appearance.

The troops next marched in a ſingle file before the Congreſs,
and M. le Chevalier de la Luzerne, miniſter from the court of
France, and afterwards encamped in a large plain contiguous to
the river Schuylkill. The next day after our arrival, the regiment
of Soiſſonnais went through the exerciſe of the fire arms: at leaſt
twenty thouſand perſons, and a vaſt number of carriages, remarkable for their lightneſs and elegance, added to the luſtre of this
exhibition, which was ſtill heightened by the pleaſantneſs of the
ſituation, and the remarkable ſerenity of the day. The rapidity
of the military evolutions, the ſoldierly appearance of the troops in
general, and the exaɛtneſs of their motions, ſurpriſed and enrap-
tured the beholders, but their attention was ſtill more excited,
when they beheld in one of our chiefs, the relation and friend of
that young *Hero* to whom they are ſo much indebted, and for whom
they profeſs an admiration ariſing almoſt to enthuſiaſm: a loſs, §
(which one muſt be a father, and of great ſenſibility too, to have a
juſt idea of) had for ſome days rendered him a prey to grief and
melancholy; not even the charms of Philadelphia could draw him
from his tent; and like another Achilles, nothing but the claſh of
arms could make him forget his ſorrow.

We were a good deal amuſed with a miſtake of ſome of the common people, who took for a great General one of thoſe alert fellows, whom our commanding officers commonly have in their reti-
nue,

§ *He had ſome days before received the news of his daughter's*
death.

nue, to run up and down to carry their written orders. His short tight bodied coat, his rich waiſtcoat with a ſilver fringe, his roſe-coloured ſhoes, his cap adorned with a coat of arms, and his cane with an enormous head,—all appeared to them ſo many tokens of extraordinary dignity. Altho' he approached his maſter, the Colonel commandant, merely to receive and publiſh his orders, they imagined that he gave them of his own accord, and directed the movements of the troops, independent of any ſuperior.

The Preſident of Congreſs,* in a ſuit of black velvet, honoured this review with his preſence. Theſe honeſt Pennſylvanians differ very conſiderably from us in the ceremonies of dreſs, as we differ from them again in our modes of legiſlation.

The manœuvres of our troops raiſed the moſt flattering expectations in the minds of the ſpectators; and they did not heſitate to declare, that ſuch ſoldiers were invincible.

This day was deſtined for favourable omens. M. le Chevalier de la Luzerne, who, upon this occaſion, received his countrymen with the dignity and generoſity of the repreſentative of a great Monarch, and the frankneſs and cordiality of an individual, after the review, invited all the officers to dine with him. Hardly were we ſeated at the table, when an expreſs arrived: a diſquieting ſilence immediately ſeized every gueſt—our eyes were fixed upon the Chevalier de la Luzerne, every one endeavouring to gueſs what the meſſage would turn out to be.————" Thirty-ſix ſhips of the " line, ſaid he, commanded by Monſieur le Comte de Graſſe, are " arrived in Cheſapeak-Bay, and three thouſand men have landed " and opened a communication with the Marquis de la Fayette."

————Joy and good humour, immediately reſumed their place on every countenance—Our impatient leaders began to count the days, and reckon how long it would be before they would have it in their power to face the enemy; and their heated imaginations made the time much ſhorter than it afterwards proved to be. Healths were next drank; and that of the Miniſter of the marine of France was not forgotten, whoſe activity and great abilities, have paved the way to the moſt brilliant ſucceſſes of our fleet: The preſence of his ſon, M. le Comte de Charlu, ſecond Colonel of the regiment of Saintonge, added ſtill more to our pleaſure and ſatisfaction.

Among others, Charles Thomſon, the Secretary of Congreſs, the ſoul of that political body, came alſo to receive and preſent his compliments. His meagre figure; furrowed countenance; his hollow ſparkling eyes: his white, ſtraight hair, that did not hang quite as low as his ears, fixed our thorough attention, and filled us with ſurprize and admiration.

The important news of the arrival of Count de Graſſe, was ſoon ſpread throughout the city, and echoes of joy were heard from every quarter: Some merry fellows mounted upon ſcaffolds and ſtages, pronounced funeral orations for Cornwallis, and

* *The Honourable Thomas M'Kean, Eſquire, was then Preſident.*

and uttered lamentations upon the grief and diftrefs of the Tories. The people ran in crowds to the refidence of the Minifter of France; and *long live Louis the Sixteenth*, was the general cry.

Thus, you fee, the people are univerfally perfuaded of the fuccefs of this expedition.—Could thefe flattering hopes be realized, they would haften a peace, which in our fituation, and under the wife and benevolent Prince that governs us, would place France in a point of view, that has been wholly unknown fince the exiftence of her monarchy.

Philadelphia, the capital of Pennfylvania, is built upon an elevated and extenfive plain, a little above the confluence, and between the two rivers, Delaware and Schuylkill. The famous William Penn, founder of this colony, gave the plan, and pointed out the fituation. His plan has been followed, but the town is built upon the principal river for the conveniency of trade. Its form is an oblong, extending two miles in length, and having eight ftreets perfectly parallel to each other, croffed at right angles by fixteen others, of near a mile in length, equally wide and as exactly parallel. Care has been taken to leave vacancies for public edifices. The two principal ftreets, *Front-ftreet*, and *Market-ftreet*, are each one hundred feet broad. Veffels of five hundred tons can lie afloat, by the moft convenient wharffs; and I faw more than twenty fhips at once upon the ftocks. The town contains at leaft fix thoufand houfes, for the moft part built of brick, and all extremely handfome; the people are computed to be about forty thoufand fouls. The Roman Catholics have two chapels here, governed by an Englifh ex-Jefuit, and a German Prieft, who reckon the number of their communicants at about eleven or twelve hundred. There are alfo churches for the Prefbyterians, Lutherans, Dutch Calvinifts, Anabaptifts, &c. but the moft numerous fect is that of the Quakers, and of this perfuafion was the founder of the colony.

As this fect pretends to more toleration, ftrictnefs of morals, and equality of condition than any other, and was eftablifhed in Pennfylvania juft after they firft attracted the notice of the European world, by the peculiarity of their religion, and at a time when the contradictions and contempt into which other perfuafions had fallen, ferved to fupport it in all its energy and aufterity; fo their legiflation tended ftill more to make thefe colonifts free, equal and fimple in their manners. The mildnefs of the climate, the goodnefs of the foil, their rural occupations, and a folitary mode of life, favoured the views of their legiflature, and Pennfylvania foon became the moft virtuous and happy colony that hiftory has ever recorded. But by the increafe of inhabitants, by the flocking in of ftrangers, and its becoming a commercial fettlement, the fortunes of individuals were enlarged, luxury was introduced, the manners of the people infenfibly changed, and that *golden age*, which was here realized, was foon confidered as nothing more than a brilliant

meteor

meteor, which blazed out a moment to the astonished world, and disappeared forever.

In this city the representatives of the thirteen States, denominated the *Congress*, hold their residence. The front of the edifice in which they sit, is of brick, and consequently without any of the orders of architecture; it is, however, as handsome as any structure in this taste can be, and presents to the eye a noble, solid, regular mass. It is placed in the common range of the houses, without any considerable interval of separation, and certainly loses much of its beauty because you have no proper stand to examine it in the requisite point of view: Each individual State sends its deputies hither to consult upon its interests, make its proposals and concert means for the defence of the common cause. This assembly has no concern with any matters further than what respects the general interest of all the States, each having its particular assembly, who make laws and provide for the support of their civil government, independent of the general Congress. The number of representatives is always in proportion to the extent and importance of the several States that send them—the fewest that can be sent are *two*, and *seven* the most, but how many soever there be, the representatives of each state have but one voice. The central position of this town, and its natural security of situation has decided the choice in its favour. The first Congress was held here the fifth of September 1774, and the act of Independence was passed July 4th, 1776; at a period, when the affairs of America looked dark and gloomy, when a very numerous fleet and army surrounded all the avenues to New-York, and threatened destruction to the very existence of liberty in America.

The market-house, situated in the midst of the city, is large and handsome. The prisons for Debtors and criminals, as well as that designed for prisoners of war, are spacious and airy.

You have heard of their Philosophical Society, of which many learned men in Europe are members. But the establishment that does the most honour to these rising States, is a Hospital intended to receive the defenders of their country, when wounds and infirmities render them incapable of providing for their own subsistence.

The plan of William Penn is yet far from being accomplished, but is perfected more and more as the town enlarges: it is easy to judge what an amazing growth it has had, when we find an old man yet alive in Philadelphia, who remembers when the very first stone of it was laid. This town, situated on a river where vessels of war may easily come up, and upon a fertile soil which requires little labour to cultivate it, and built after a well considered plan, cannot fail of becoming in time one of the largest and most beautiful cities in the world   I am, &c.

LETTER

LETTER VIII. *The army arrives at the Head of Elk.—Embarkation of several regiments at that place.—The main body proceed on.—Baltimore described.—Of the Acadians, or French neutrals, settled there.—Their ministers, religious discipline &c.—The unsettled state of the churches in Maryland and Virginia.*

Baltimore, September 14, 1781.

WHEN the army reached the Head of Elk, a place on the north of Chesapeak bay, we had the mortification to find there was not a sufficiency of transports to receive us all on board: It was with difficulty that we could even procure shallops and boats, for the most part open, to take in the grenadiers, chasseurs and some American regiments: in case of bad weather these troops will suffer much and run a considerable risk of being drowned; General Washington and Count Rochambeau, have advanced on by land, to concert their plans of operation with M. de Graffe. M. le Baron de Viomenil, the immediate commander of the French army, has determined likewise to go all the way by land.

Baltimore is, from its situation, one of the most important places of all North-America.—Placed almost at the head of the Bay, it lies convenient to receive the produce of Pennsylvania, the Delaware state, and especially the commodities of Maryland. This last mentioned state has very considerable iron forges, and produces a species of tobacco of a less pleasing smell than that of Virginia, but infinitely more strong, and for that reason preferred by the people of the north of Europe.

Thirty years ago, Baltimore was only an inconsiderable village ; at present it is a large wealthy town, built nearly in the shape of a crescent or half-moon, The northern part of it, is situated upon a narrow slip of land, that projects a considerable distance into the Bay, and is so low, that the town in this place, apparently rises out of the bosom of the waters, and already seems to anticipate its future dominion and grandeur.

Lord Baltimore, an Irish Catholic, formerly established two hundred of his persuasion in this place, and gave his name to the settlement. About one quarter of it is peopled by those unfortunate Acadians, and their descendents, whom the English cruelly forced away from their own happy country,‡ to leave them destitute and
poor

‡ *The best of Nova Scotia is that part called by the French* Acadia, *where a number of that nation first settled in* 1604. *These people were known by the name of* Neutrals, *and lived in a perfect State of independence after the Province was given up to England, having sworn never to act against their native country, to which, as well as to their religion and priests, they were most enthusiastically attached. Soon after the year* 1749, *perceiving the English encroach-*

poor in a region where they were utter ftrangers. Their quarter is the meaneft in appearance, and worft built of all, and the tyranny of the Britifh government has, till lately, hindered them from gaining any thing by the happy fituation of this town; but being for the moft part fea-faring men it is hoped they will not fail, in time, to make up by commerce the lofs of their fertile fettlements in Acadia.

They ftill preferve the French language among them, and are prodigioufly attached to whatever regards the nation from which they originated, efpecially in their religious worfhip, which they keep up with a ftrictnefs that would have done honour to the primitive ages of chriftianity. Their way of life is plain and fimple, and their manners fimilar to thofe prevalent among them while they were yet in the happy region of Acadia. The priefts there exercifed that authority over them which virtue and education allow, over men who are not yet corrupt in their morals, they were their judges and their mediators, and to this day thefe exiled people never mention their names without tears.

They told me a great deal about a *Monfieur le Clerc*, who, at their departure, gave them veffels and ornaments for the fervice of the altar. " Thefe ornaments (faid the good old man) will ferve " to recall to your minds what you owe to the religion of your " fathers: can it flourifh—can it even exift in thofe new regions " which you are now going to inhabit! While you reprove all " other creeds and modes of worfhip, can you fhow by your gen- " tlenefs, good will and beneficence, that you ftill hold them " as brethren, who are of a different faith! Perhaps Providence is " making you its inftruments to extend the divine truths of the " gofpel, and render them prevalent in fome other region of the " world. This reflection alone fupports me under the forrow and " pangs of parting, but wherever you may be forced by the will of " heaven, rely upon it, my heart will always follow you, and " never, never will I raife my trembling hands to the facred " altars of the Divinity, but you fhall be the deareft objects of my " prayers."

Their chapel is built without the town upon a height, near four or five churches of different fects. They complain much, that they do not find in their prefent minifters, the zeal and affection of thofe in Acadia: taken up with their temporal concerns, they beftow few inftructions upon their flock, and their whole paftoral function feems confined to faying low mafs once a month.

G   When

ing upon them, they determined rather to remove to New France (Canada) than run the rifque of having their religion contaminated by an intermixture with heretics. But the Englifh getting notice of their defign, feized upon all who were not yet gone, and embarked them on board their fhips, in which they were tranfported to different parts of the then Englifh Colonies, where the greater part of them foon died of grief and vexation.

When they faw a French clergyman, it feemed to revive the idea of their former paftors. They even urged me to officiate in their church, and while I was performing that facred duty in compliance with their requeft, I could not but congratulate them upon their piety, and lay before them a pattern of the virtues of their fathers; I recalled to their minds the long-vanifhed ideas of thofe much refpected perfons, and they immediately diffolved into tears ; the mufic too, which I had introduced upon this occafion, contributed its fhare to melt and move their hearts.

Maryland has a great proportion of catholics among its inhabitants. At Frederickfburg and other places in Virginia there are feveral churches, as well as at Charleftown, the capital of South-Carolina. All the North-American churches were under the jurifdiction of the bifhop of London, who fince the Revolution, however, has relinquifhed all connexion with them, proteftants as well as papifts, and they are now left to themfelves, without head and without unity. The religion and number of thefe people ought neverthelefs to claim the attention of the patrons of the church.——   I am, &c.

LETTER IX. *The combined armies embark at Annapolis for York in Virginia.—Difference of the manners and cuftoms, in the Northern and Southern States.*

Annapolis, September 21, 1781.

THE army was to profecute the reft of the march to Virginia by land, and with that view took the road leading to *Alexandria,* a flourifhing commercial town upon the Potomack; but upon the news of the arrival of the Romulus fhip of war, with two frigates and a number of tranfports, we turned off towards Annapolis, but the horfes and carriages continued their journey by land.

As we advance towards the fouth we obferve a fenfible difference in the manners and cuftoms of the people. We no longer find, as in Connecticut, houfes fituated along the road at fmall diftances, juft large enough to contain a fingle family, and the houfhold furniture nothing more than is barely neceffary ; here are fpacious habitations, confifting of different buildings, at fome diftance from each other, furrounded with plantations that extend beyond the reach of the eye, cultivated not by the hands of freemen, but by thofe unhappy blacks, whom European avarice and injuftice has taken from their native regions of Africa to cultivate poffeffions not their own, in a foreign foil. Their furniture here, is conftructed out of the moft coftly kinds of wood, and the moft valuable marble, enriched by the elegant devices of the artifts hand. Their riding machines are light and handfome, and drawn by the fleeteft couriers, managed by flaves richly dreffed : this

opulence

opulence was particularly obfervable at *Annapolis*. That very inconfiderable town, ftanding at the mouth of the river *Severn*, where it falls into the bay, out of the few buildings it contains, has at leaft three fourths, fuch as may be ftiled elegant and grand. Female luxury here exceeds what is known in the provinces of France: a French hair dreffer is a man of importance among them, and it is faid, a certain dame here hires one of that craft at a thoufand crowns a year falary. The ftate-houfe is a very beautiful building, I think the moft fo of any I have feen in America. The periftyle is fet off with pillars, and the edifice is topped with a dome.

We are embarking with the greateft expedition ; the weather is the fineft you can conceive, and the wind fair : I think the impatience of the French will foon be at an end.

I am, &c.

LETTER X. *Arrival of the troops at James-Town.—Wil-liamfburg—Its State Houfe—College, Library and Profeffors.— Climate of Virginia—Tobacco—Commerce—Population—Condi-tion of the Slaves—Rivers of the Country—Trees and Plants—A curious fpecies of the Catterpillar—Dangerous effects from the fling of a Spider—Petrifactions common in Virginia.*

Williamfburgh, September 30, 1781.

THE army has had a very agreeable paffage hither, except the grenadiers, chaffeurs, and the firft American regiments, who were fourteen days on the water. Judge how inconvenient this muft have been to troops crowded into a narrow fpace, and without any decks over them ; while even the officers had nothing but bifcuit to live upon. The fhores of this Bay, which is formed by the influx of fo many great rivers, are far from being lofty, neither are they much cleared of the woods, and it is but rarely that you difcover any habitations ; but the few we faw were very agreeably fituated. This country will be, in time, one of the moft beautiful in the world.

When our little fleet had failed up James-River, celebrated for the excellent tobacco which grows upon its fhores, we difembark-ed at James-Town, the place where the Englifh firft eftablifhed themfelves in Virginia. The troops have already joined the grena-diers, chaffeurs, and the three thoufand men brought hither by Count de Graffe, confifting of the regiments of *Agenois, Gatinois* and *Touraine*, under the command of Monf. de St. Simon, Mare-chal de Camp. This General had a little before, effected a junc-tion with fifteen hundred or two thoufand Americans, commanded
by

* *Thefe failed from the Head of Elk.*

by M. le Marquis de la Fayette, who, as you have heard, could never be reduced, notwithstanding the forces of Cornwallis were three or four times his number. I should have mentioned, that M. de la Fayette, in quality of Major-General of an American army, at the age of twenty-four years, found himself at this time superior in command to a French general officer, and continued so till the other detachments of the army were collected into one body, under General Washington.

Williamsburg, tho' considerable, as the capital of Virginia, is in other respects a place of little importance : it is situated upon a plain, level piece of land, and the main street, passing through the midst of it, is more than one hundred feet in width ; at one of the extremities, and fronting the street is the capitol, or state-house, a small but regular building ; and at the other end is the college, capable of containing more than three hundred students : there is a library belonging to it of about three thousand volumes, and an apparatus for experimental philosophy, tolerably complete. With the most lively satisfaction I contemplated these monuments of the real glory of men ; and while I contemplated them, they recalled to my mind places and persons most intimately connected with my heart. The tumult of arms has driven from hence, those who had the care of these philosophical instruments, for the muses you know, take no pleasure but in the abodes of peace : We could only meet with one solitary professor, of Italian extraction ; and I cannot but say, his conversation and abilities appeared to be such, that after what he had told us in commendation of his brethren, we could not help regretting their absence.

Williamsburg does not contain above a hundred and fifty houses, and is the only town we have yet seen in Virginia worth mentioning; not situated on the banks of any river, it stands at an equal distance from two small ones, one of which falls into York, the other into James River. It is subject to the inconveniency of scarcity of good water. What makes the situation of this place valuable, is the neighbourhood of James and York rivers, between which grows the best tobacco in the whole State, and for this reason it seems to have been built where it is: I do not think, nevertheless, that it will ever be a place of any great importance ; the towns of York, James, Norfolk, and Edenton, being more favourably situated for trade, will undoubtedly eclipse it.

Although Virginia extends from the 36th. to the 39th. degree of north latitude, the winters are very severe, and great quantities of snow sometimes fall. The southern and eastern winds are excessive warm, and those from the north and west, coming over mountains and lakes, equally cold. In a days time there will often be a rapid transition from one extreme to the other. The country produces several very excellent kinds of wood, and about Williamsburg and the shores of the bay, the land is covered with trees yielding rozin; the meadows and marshes subsist great numbers of excellent horses, which far exceed those of the other States in point

of

of beauty: Vaſt quanties of hemp are raiſed here, as well as flax, Indian corn and cotton: The cotton ſhrubs produce annually, and at the firſt view we took them for beans in bloſſom. Silk worms ſucceed here very well, and it is not improbable but they may at ſome future time form one of the moſt conſiderable branches of trade in this ſtate. The commodity moſt in demand is tobacco ; you well know the character it has, and for common uſe it may be conſidered as the beſt in the world: What the Engliſh imported yearly from this ſtate, and from Maryland, might have amounted to about ninety-ſix thouſand hogſheads ; but among themſelves they did not conſume one ſixth part of that quantity, and either diſpoſed of the reſt among us, or exported it to the north ; judge then how valuable this commerce was to that nation. They purchaſed it here at the very loweſt rate, taking it in exchange for their broadcloths, linen and hard wares, and ſelling again for ready money what they did not want for their own home conſumption, and thus they increaſed their capital every year to the amount of eight or nine millions. No other of their poſſeſſions, not even thoſe in India, ever afforded them ſo clear a profit. Three hundred and thirty veſſels, and about four thouſand ſailors were conſtantly employed in this trade : of theſe the city of Glaſgow, in Scotland, owned the greateſt part, and by that means ſupported its flouriſhing manufactures, which were perhaps more conſiderable than thoſe of any town in England.

Since the war, the tobacco exportation has been only about forty thouſand hogſheads annually ; what advantages then would have accrued to the Engliſh, could they have ſooner made themſelves maſters of Cheſapeake-bay. There are now fifty or ſixty veſſels collected at York, under the cannon of Cornwallis, ſent on purpoſe to load with this weed, which three fourths and a half of the human race take ſuch ſupreme delight in chewing, ſnuffing or ſmoking.

The population of Virginia, is computed at one hundred and fifty thouſand whites, and five hundred thouſand negroes. There is a ſtill greater diſproportion between the whites and blacks in Maryland, where there are not more than twenty thouſand whites, and at leaſt two hundred thouſand negroes. The Engliſh imported into theſe two provinces, between ſeven and eight thouſand yearly. Perhaps the lot of theſe ſlaves is not quite ſo hard as that of the negroes in the Iſlands ; their liberty, it is true, is irreparably loſt in both places, but here they are treated with more mildneſs, and are ſupported upon the ſame kind of food with their maſters ; and if the earth which they cultivate, is moiſtened with their ſweat, it has never been known to bluſh with their blood. The American, not at all induſtrious by nature, is conſiderate enough not to expect too much from his ſlave, who in ſuch circumſtances, has fewer motives to be laborious than himſelf.

The great rivers, which water this province, have their ſource in the blue mountains, a chain of which runs through the whole country, from north to ſouth. Beyond theſe rolls the Ohio, through vaſt foreſts and meadows, in a ſerpentine courſe, till it unites with

the

the Miffifippi : according to the reports of travellers, the fineft and moft fertile countries in the world extend along the fhores of this river, which are neverthelefs as yet but ill explored. It is faid, that General Wafhington had in contemplation, if he could not break the chains of his country, to go and eftablifh himfelf there with thofe, whom the love of liberty and independence fhould incline to partake of his fate and fortune.

As you advance to the fouthward, the different degrees of heat are obfervable by the difference of the vegetable productions. The gum-laurel rifes here into a tree, and the faffafras becomes tall and ftately. We took notice in Maryland, of a fruit very common there, fharp tafted and bitterifh before it was ripe, but, like our forb apples, lufcious, infipid and flabby, when come to maturity, being about the bignefs of a plumb, and of a bright yellow.

Almoft all the plants here are odoriferous : the white *flower-ever-lafting*, of which the fields are full, is remarkably fo. The catterpillars differ entirely from thofe of Europe, being covered with tufts, which hide both their heads and feet: thefe tufts are long, clofe and fmooth as if they had been trimmed with fciffors ; fome are all over of one colour, fuch as a very fine vermillion, others are chequered with regular fpots.

We found near the North-River, in the ftate of New-York, another fpecies of this infect, remarkable for its fize and beauty. M. le Chevalier de Chattelux,* whom the great affairs of an army do not entirely preclude from allotting fome moments to literary amufement, made me a prefent of one, which I have delineated upon paper : it was about four inches long, and had feven or eight rings paffing round the body ; its fkin was thin and of a light green, through which you might perceive the motion of the blood in the arteries; his eye-balls were about the bignefs of a pea, and his tail of a deep yellow ; each of his rings had four little branchy horns, hard and of a jet black, about two twelfths of an inch long : his head was armed with eight more, more than an inch in length, ftrong, branchy, and bent towards each other, yellow, and black towards the extremities, and polifhed in the moft exquifite manner. This ftately infect lets us know, by the arrogance of its carriage, that it is not ignorant of the noble drefs it wears, and feems confcious of a natural fuperiority over its fellow worms.

I have had a dangerous trial of the wonderful fubtlety of the poifon of a fpecies of the fpider; it ftung me in the forehead as I was going to bed in my tent, but I hardly felt any pain in the fpot where the fting had penetrated, and the pimple it occafioned was barely perceptible: however, fome fhootings in the mufcles of my throat on the fide next to the wound, prevented me from getting any fleep: in half an hour afterwards I found my belly was fwollen, and my body full of dead, heavy pains. I then got up and walked

* M. le Chevalier de Chattelux, Marechal de Camp, one of the forty members of the French academy, is Major-General in the army of Count Rochambeau.

walked about in the open air, but my pains increasing rapidly, communicated themselves to my back, and at length centered in my stomach ; In a short time I could support myself no longer on my legs, and in this condition was carried to Williamsburg, from which we were only a few hundreds of yards distant: here they gave me some volatile alkaline salts, and rubbed the part where I had been stung ; but notwithstanding this, the oppression at my stomach increased, and my pains became more and more violent; bleeding was of little or no service, and I was relieved at last by the simple remedy of warm water, which had I delayed to make use of, I should infallibly have died for want of breath. As the nervous system was only attacked by the poison, it is plain the alkaline salts could but have increased the irritation. I am now recovered, except that I have at times some painful shootings in my nerves, * a kind of malady I could hardly give credit to, were I not actually the sufferer.

In Maryland, I began to pick up petrified shell-fish, where there is great plenty on the shores of the bay, but in the neighbourhood of Williamsburg I have seen the ground guttured out to the depth of more than twenty-five feet by the land floods, and disclosing vast quantities of these substances, the greater part of which was not more than half petrified.

The army is at present before York. We hear the reports of the cannon very distinctly; and I am now going to join the troops, where I think I shall shortly have something very interesting to impart to you.   I am, &c.

LETTER XI. *The combined Forces march from Williamsburg.*
York invested.— Various preparatory operations of the army. ——
Batteries opened upon the town.—The Charon burnt.—Distressed
situation of Lord Cornwallis.—Tarleton's expedition.—repulsed by
the Duke de Lauzun.— Reflexions upon sieges and battles.— A party
of the besieged surprise a French battery.——Lord Cornwallis
endeavours to escape in the night to Glocester.—Prevented by bad
weather.—Sends out a flag.— Offers to capitulate.—The articles of
surrender.—Mutual hatred betwixt the English and the Americans.
Destruction of the town of York from the cannonading.—The troops
go into winter quarters.

Camp at York, November 6, 1781.

THE combined army left Williamsburg the 28th of September, with a view to invest York ; and advanced the same day
to

---

* *Since my return to France I have had several touches of these pains in my nerves.*

to within three quarters of a league of the town. Such approaches as these are not commonly made without great circumspection, since the encampments must necessarily be multiplied in proportion as you draw near to the enemy, but the impatience of the troops for action rendered them rather too venturesome on this occasion, not hesitating to march twelve miles in the face of the enemy through dangerous woods, upon a loose, sandy soil, and through the most excessive heats. One of our young Colonels went so far, as to use every argument he could think of to prevail upon General Washington to suffer him to attack two redoubts that lay in our way. The General referred the matter to M. le Comte de Rochambeau, to whom he had intrusted the immediate direction of the siege, but Count Rochambeau thought it more prudent to give the troops a little time for repose, and reconnoitre the places, before he made any attempt of that kind.

A body of Americans, headed by the Marquis de la Fayette, composed the right column, and the French, preceded by their grenadiers and chasseurs formed the left. The army of M. le Compte de Rochambeau, consisting of the regiments of *Bourbonnais*, *Royal Deux Ponts*, *Soissonnais* and *Saintonge* was placed in the center: The troops under the command of *M. de Saint Simon* extended to the left as far as *York* river, and the Americans occupied the right, flanked by the same river.

On the thirtieth, the enemy evacuated the two redoubts, which the young Colonel was for attacking upon our first arrival: they were distant about four hundred toises [eight hundred yards] from their main works, and upon their leaving them, the French immediately took possession.

On the first of October in the night, the Americans began two redoubts to the right of the others. The enemy discovering this, instantly turned their fire that way, and as we expected, several of the American workmen were killed. This, however, did not at all intimidate their companions, who held on at their business with the same ardour as if no such accident had happened. §

The army was busy, till the sixth, in constructing long and short fascines, gabions, and landing the Artillery and ammunition. We were soon after in a situation to open the trenches. The regiments of Bourbonnais and Soissonnais, commanded by Baron de Viomenil, and fifteen hundred Americans under the Marquis de la Fayette, posted themselves all night in a deep ravine to protect the fifteen hundred workmen on the right. At the same time the regiment de Touraine opened the intrenchment on the left, and raised a battery over against a redoubt, detached from their main works, and intended to keep off the fire directed from the right of the enemy. The activity of the workmen and the natural loose-
nets

§ *These were militia men, to whom the siege was a spectacle altogether new.*

nefs of the foil, to our great aftonifhment, put the parallel into a
ftate to receive the troops on the next day.   They entered it about
noon, with drums beating.

The opening of the trenches, which is ordinarily the moft fatal
period of a fiege, was in this inftance executed without the effufion
of blood; a circumftance the more fortunate, as the wounded
would have been unprovided with ftraw to lie on, and linen rags
for the dreffing of their wounds.   This was performed on the
7th: on the 8th and 9th they laboured hard in conftructing
batteries, which were profecuted with fuch expedition that thofe of
the Americans and Monfieur de Saint Simon opened about five in
the evening.   The latter foon forced a frigate to move from her
moorings, that had been very troublefome in firing upon our encampments; they alfo levelled a red hot ball at the Charon, a
forty-four gun fhip, and burnt her, as they did likewife a floop.
The batteries of Count Rochambeau began to play on the tenth,
at feven in the morning; and now the difference of the two firings
could eafily be diftinguifhed; that of the enemy was flow and
irregular, while ours was brifk and well fupported.   Our engineers
had pitched upon the moft advantageous pofitions, and the artillery men made every difcharge take effect by the exactnefs of their
aim, and their alertnefs in working the guns.

Lord Cornwallis had not prepared his troops for fuch falutations
as thefe; he had affured them, on the contrary, " that we were
unprovided with battering cannon, and had only fome field pieces;
that our troops were raw and unfkilled in war, and that thofe of M.
de Saint Simon in particular, were nothing better than undifciplined vagabonds, collected in the Weft Indies, enervated by a hot
climate, and would foon be conquered, were it only by the firft
attacks of the cold weather, prevalent in thefe countries: and as
to the American troops, they knew very well what diftreffed circumftances they were in; and finally, that powerful fuccours
from New-York would foon put them in a fituation to befiege the
befiegers."

This harangue did but increafe their confternation.   As foon as
they began to hear the terrible roaring of our batteries, we that
were on the heights faw them flying precipitately from their
redoubts, while their batteries in an inftant were entirely filenced.
They had been quiet fpectators of our labours, and we now became
fo in our turn with refpect to them.   At this time I watched an
opportunity to traverfe our lines, which confifted of a large ditch,
broad enough for carriages to travel in, about four feet in depth,
and covered by a rampart of gabions, or cylindrical bafkets, fixed
upon the ground, by means of projecting ftakes, filled and covered
over with loofe dirt, and forming a height of about feven feet on
the fide towards the enemy.   The batteries were placed upon
platforms, on the infide of the ditch, raifed and ftrengthened with
palifadoes.   The quarter next the enemy was covered by a large
parapet, in which were the embrafures for the cannon: all thefe

works, as well as most of those of the English consisted wholly of earth.

I now beheld the cannon, those infernal machines, playing with the utmost fury; I saw the rapid bullet striking or rebounding from the redoubts of the enemy, and driving thro' the air the planks and timber, which formed the embrasures for the great guns. * I followed with my eye, in its parabolic path, the slow and destructive bomb, sometimes burying itself in the roofs of houses, sometimes when it burst, raising clouds of dust and rubbish from the ruins of the buildings, at other times blowing the unfortunate wretches, that happened to be within its reach, more than twenty feet high in the air, and letting them fall at a considerable distance most pitiably torn. Such terrible sights as these fix and captivate the attention, and fill the mind at the same instant with trouble, wonder and consternation. " The besieged, (said the deserters) are in the utmost confusion; not knowing where to fly, death seizes them even in the arms of sleep: and the General, uneasy at the discontent of the Hessians, no longer confides his advanced guard to any but the English soldiers."

We had to pass to our entrenchments through a narrow defile, where the enemy principally directed their fire, and the first lodgment for such as should chance to be wounded was but a small distance-off. I advanced thither as fast as my health and strength would permit, and perceived that the bullets often fell upon the fascine cabbin in which we were. I here observed, in the dead of night, the different degrees of celerity betwixt the flash, the sound, and the projected body. The light preceded the sound, and the sound the stroke, but at a much less considerable interval of time.

Tarleton, that impetuous leader, who had spread terror through their whole march from Carolina, on the day that the batteries of Count Rochambeau began to play made a sally by way of Glocester, at the head of his legion consisting of four hundred picked men. M. le Choisi, Brigadier General, then marched against him with a part of his troops, who together with M. le Duc de Lauzun, at the head of his Hussars, repulsed him with the loss of about fifty of his men: this event was a thunder stroke to the inhabitants of the country, who had hitherto believed Tarleton invincible, and formed a judgment of his talents from the boldness of his thefts and robberies.

In the night of the eleventh we opened a second parallel, at about three hundred yards from the enemy's main works: a prodigious quantity of royal grenades, or small bombs, from the enemy disturbed the workmen a good deal, which did not however prevent them from going on with alacrity; but we now relaxed the fire of our artillery for fear of doing them damage by our shot, as well

* *Ours were made of fascines, and consequently were less exposed to be damaged by the fire of the enemy.*

well as becaufe we began to demolifh our old batteries to conftruct new ones. At this time the fire of the enemy became brifker than ufual.

True bravery manifefts itfelf chiefly in fieges. The confufion, the hurry, the example of others, all contribute during a battle, to roufe, move and animate the moft timid, who, in an inftant become fuperior to themfelves : but in the long continued fatigues of a fiege, where dangers are inceffantly growing out of each other, where, in the filence and folitude of darknefs we have to face death with coolnefs and unconcern, to reflect on its confequences and horrors with calmnefs, and fet the real lofs of life in competition with the uncertainty of our hopes and expectations in a ftate of futurity, then it is that the courage of a warrior proves itfelf to fpring from an unbounded love of honour, and an invincible attachment to his duty.

The French, in this fiege, feemed to become rivals to each other; and each officer envied the lot of him who was fent upon attempts of the greateft danger ; they hurried away, with a curiofity which I cannot but call rafhnefs and madnefs, to examine the works of the enemy, and haften the progrefs of our own. Even the obfcure common foldier, whofe life and death is equally configned to oblivion, ftrove to outdo his renowned officers in thefe daring enterprizes, and went up in defiance of the enemy to the very edges of their intrenchments. The miner, with the axe in his hand, advanced with a determined ftep through a fhower of grape-fhot to cut down the tree at his leifure, which perhaps fhielded him from deftruction. The corps of artillery, fo diftinguifhed by the abilities and intrepidity of their officers, were no lefs fo by the activity, fpirit and courage of their foldiery.* General Wafhington himfelf beheld the effects of this daring fpirit with aftonifhment ; a bomb or a bullet, fortunately pointed, excited in them the lively emotions of an eager huntfman, who is upon the point of feizing his prey.

A gunner, at one of the embrafures, had his foot carried away by a bullet. I tried to confole the unhappy man in the firft moments of his anguifh, when he gave me for anfwer,—" I am lefs afflicted for the lofs of my foot, than for being fo unfortunate as not to have had time, before it happened, to difcharge the cannon I had pointed with fo much care !"—He foon after died of his wound, and never ceafed to complain, till the laft, of the failure he had made in firing the piece.

As

* *The foldiers of thefe corps, are no way inferior to the others in bravery, capacity, and a fondnefs for doing their duty. I muft confefs they are not fo fatigued by conftant exercife, nor fubjected to fo fevere a difcipline as the others, and therefore if the fame ends can be accomplifhed by more fimple methods, lefs fatiguing to the officers, and lefs hard upon the foldiers, why fhould we hefitate to prefer that mode which is the eafieft ?*

As long as we were working at the batteries of the second parallel, the fire of the enemy was inceffantly kept up. The works, that were carried on with the greateft vigour, were not, however, extended as far as the affailants wifhed. They demanded, with vehement exclamations, to be led on to attack the two detached redoubts, which incommoded them much, and the poffeffion of which, would enable them to enfilade a part of the works of the enemy : The eager valour of the Baron de Viomenil, was particularly impatient of reftraint in this enterprize, when, at length, on the 14th, he was ordered to attack one of them, having under him Count William de Deux Ponts, fecond Colonel of the regiment of Royal Deux Ponts, and M. le Chevalier de Lameth, Aide-Marechal : The Marquis de la Fayette commanded the attack upon the other, and M. de Gimat was placed under his direction — both redoubts were taken fword in hand ; but unfortuately Count William was wounded, and the Chevalier de Lameth mortally in both his knees.

The following night four hundred of the befieged, pretending to be Americans, furprifed one of our batteries, nailed up feven pieces of cannon, killed fome foldiers, made a few prifoners, and wounded about thirty; a lad of fifteen years old, fervant to an officer, who was fleeping juft by, was ftabbed with a bayonet in thirteen or fourteen different parts of his body. The regiment of Soiffonnais, which was pofted a fmall diftance off, knew nothing of this affair till it was over, becaufe the officer who commanded the redoubt had given orders not to fire, or make an alarm at the approach of thefe pretended Americans; this regiment, however, foon haftened up, and had not the Lieutenant Colonel of Saintonge founded a retreat, the Englifh would have been completely furrounded. Several of the enemies foldiers were wounded and brought to our hofpitals, and the men who a moment before had been cutting each others throats, were now collected under the fame roof, and received, indifcriminately, the fame care and attention. And thus it is, that in the midft of the horrors that diftrefs and difgrace our nature, there are ftill fome traces left of the once noble and exalted difpofition of mankind.

On the fixteenth and feventeenth, our new batteries began to play; broke fome pallifadoes, and even made a breach in the enemy's works. Lord Cornwallis finding himfelf upon the point of being torn and crufhed from every quarter, now took the defperate refolution of paffing over in the night to Glocefter, a poft ftill lefs capable of defence than York. Bad weather, however, hindered him from accomplifhing his purpofe, and on the feventeenth, at ten in the morning, he fent a flag to afk a ceffation of arms for twenty-four hours: the deputies were reminded of the behaviour of their Generals at Charleftown and Savannah in fimilar circumftances, and had their requeft refufed. Another flag then came out propofing a furrender, when two hours fufpenfion of arms was granted them, which term was afterwards prolonged.

Lord

Lord Cornwallis defired to know what terms of capitulation were to be allowed him.——" THOSE OF CHARLESTOWN," anfwered General Wafhington, with fpirit and judgment.

By thus recalling a victory to their remembrance, in which they had manifefted the moft overbearing infolence, he taught them to treat the Americans in a different manner, for the time to come, when they fhould happen to fall under their power. M. le Vicomte de Noailles and Mr. Laurens, an American officer of great merit, fon of that Prefident of Congrefs, who was fo long in the tower of London, acted as commiffioners on this occafion. The firft requeft the Englifh deputies made was to know the names of our chief Engineers and officers of artillery ; for they declared, that it was not in the power of man to point out perfons poffeffed of greater talents or fkill in their profeffion.

On the eighteenth of October, about noon, the articles of Capitulation were figned, and on the nineteenth, Lord Cornwallis and his army furrendered themfelves prifoners of war.——

ARTICLES *of Capitulation agreed upon between his excellency General Wafhington, Count Rochambeau and Count de Graffe on the one part; and the right Honourable Earl Cornwallis, Lieutenant General of the forces of his Britannic Majefty, commanding the garrifons at York in Virginia, of the other part.*

Article 1. The garrifons of York and Glocefter, including the officers and failors of the fhips of his Britannic Majefty, as well as the marines, fhall furrender themfelves prifoners of war to the combined forces of America and France. The land forces fhall be prifoners to the United States, and the marine fhall belong to the fleet of his moft Chriftian Majefty.

2. The Artillery, arms and cloathing, the military treafure and the public magazines of what kind foever, fhall be given up without wafte or diminution, to the chiefs of the different departments, that fhall be appointed to receive them.

3. To day, at noon, the two redoubts upon the left flank of York fhall be delivered up, one to a detachment of the American army, the other to a detachment of the French grenadiers. The garrifon fhall march out to the place to be agreed upon, in the front of the army, with their mufquets on their fhoulders, the drums beating an Englifh or German march, and the colours in their cafes. They fhall there depofit their arms and return to their encampments; where they will remain till they fhall depart for the place of their deftination. The two works at Glocefter fhall be delivered up at the fame time to two detachments of French and American troops, that fhall be fent to take poffeffion of them, and the garrifon fhall march out at three this afternoon, the cavalry with their fwords drawn and trumpets founding, and the infantry

will

will file off in the manner prescribed to the garrison of York, and return to their encampment till such times as they shall be finally marched off to the place appointed.

4. The officers shall retain their swords, and both officers and soldiers shall keep their private property of every kind; no part of their baggage nor papers shall be liable to be searched or examined; and such baggage and papers, belonging to the officers, as were taken during the siege, shall be kept safe for them. *It is to be understood that the property of the inhabitants of this State, which shall be visibly in the hands of the garrison may be reclaimed.* *

5. The soldiery shall remain in Virginia, Maryland or Pennsylvania, and shall be distributed by regiments as much as possible: they will receive the same rations as the American soldiers; and an officer of each nation, English, Anspach or Hessian, and other officers upon their parole, in the proportion of one to fifty men, shall have liberty to reside near their respective regiments, to visit them often, and be witnesses of their treatment: the officers will receive and distribute the cloathing and other necessaries, and passports shall be granted for them whenever they are demanded. The General, those in civil offices, and other officers not employed as mentioned in the foregoing article, and who shall desire it, shall have permission to go to New-York upon their parole, to England, or any American post, actually in the possession of the English forces, as they shall see fit

6. The Count de Grasse shall supply the necessary vessels to carry them to New-York, in ten days, reckoning from the date of these articles, by way of flag of truce, and they shall remain in a place to be agreed upon, till they are ready to embark. The officers of the civil department of the army and marine, are included in this article: and passports by land shall be given those who cannot be furnished with vessels to go by water.

7. The

---

* *This last clause of the article caused great difficulty on the part of the English. The simple supposition that they had plundered the inhabitants was humiliating; if it was proved, it would be dishonourable. This motive, as well as the novelty of the sight, was the occasion of many thousands of Americans flocking down to see the surrender of York. Their most important object was the negroes. There have been several anecdotes handed about relative to reclaimed property, one of which bears rather hard upon Tarleton. He sat out one day to dine with one of our commanding officers, and was mounted upon a very fine horse, accompanied by several French Aids de Camp. An American instantly appeared and claimed his horse, ran up, stopped him and obliged the Colonel to dismount, loading him at the same time with the most bitter invectives. Somebody then lent him a very mean beast, upon which he arrived among our officers, who were utterly at a loss to contrive how a man of so much spirit could endure to be so humbly mounted.*

7. The officers fhall be permitted to keep foldiers with them in quality of fervants, according to the common ufage of the army: thofe fervants who are not foldiers, are not to be confidered as prifoners of war, and may go with their mafters.

8. The Bonetta floop of war fhall be fitted for fea, and retained by her former captain and crew, and left wholly to the difpofal of Lord Cornwallis, from the moment the Capitulation fhall be figned. She fhall take on board an Aid de Camp to carry difpatches to Sir Henry Clinton. The foldiers that he fhall judge proper to fend to New-York may go off without being examined, whenever his difpatches fhall be ready: his Lordfhip will engage on his part that the veffel fhall be reftored to the orders of Count de Graffe if fhe efcapes the dangers of the fea, and that he will not carry off any public property in her, and will keep an account of the number of the foldiers and crew that fhall be wanting on her return, and which he engages to account for.

9. The merchants to retain their effects, and fhall be allowed three months to difpofe of their property, or carry it away, and are not to be confidered as prifoners of war.—(Anfwer)—the merchants may fell their effects, the allied army to have the firft right of purchafe. (The merchants to be held prifoners of war.)

10. The natives or inhabitants of the different parts of the country, at prefent in York and Glocefter, are not to be punifhed for having joined the Englifh army—Anfwer—This article cannot be agreed to, as it is wholly a matter of civil concern.

11. Hofpitals fhall be furnifhed for the fick and wounded; who fhall be attended by their own furgeons on parole, and furnifhed with medicines and provifions from the American ftores—Anfwer—The Hofpital ftores, at prefent in York and Glocefter, fhall be given up for the ufe of the fick and wounded of the Englifh; and they fhall have paffports to procure fupplies from New-York, as occafion fhall require; and proper hofpitals fhall be furnifhed for receiving the fick and wounded of both garrifons.

12. Waggons fhall be provided to carry the baggage of fuch officers as fhall remain with the foldiers, as well as the furgeons, when travelling for the purpofe of recovering the fick, and wounded: and this fhall be at the public expence.

13. The fhips and boats in both harbours fhall be delivered up with all their ftores, guns and tackle, in the condition they now are, to an officer of the French marine who fhall be appointed for that purpofe; firft unloading the property of individuals, which had been put on board for fecurity during the fiege.

14. No article of this capitulation to be violated under pretence of reprifal; if there are any dubious expreffions in it, they are to be explained according to the common form and import of the words.

Done at York, in Virginia, October 18, 1781.

Signed, Cornwallis; —— Thomas Symonds.

The

The nineteenth about four in the afternoon, the Englifh and Heffians filed off, with their colours cafed, betwixt the French and American armies, at the head of which were General Wafhington and Count Rochambeau: the garrifon at Glocefter marched out before the troops of M. de Choifi. Lord Cornwallis pretended ficknefs, to avoid appearing on this occafion, and it was faid, he gave himfelf up entirely to vexation and defpair: indeed it was no wonder, for he now faw the fruit of many years fuccefs vanifh in a moment; the painful, laborious march he had made through the defert, half peopled region of North-Carolina, in order to conquer Virginia, was now entirely loft. An army, by whom he was almoft adored, confifting of more than feven thoufand choice troops, were obliged to furrender their arms to an enemy as much depifed as hated; twelve thoufand mufquets, more than two hundred pieces of Iron and Brafs cannon, and a prodigious quantity of warlike ftores were now transferred into hands that would inevitably turn them to the difadvantage of his country; he moreover faw their marine deprived at once of fifteen hundred failors and fixty fquare-rigged veffels, exclufive of a fhip of forty-four guns and two frigates, befides the total lofs of the commercial productions of Virginia.

The two lines of the combined army were more than a mile in length; the Americans were to the right: but the difproportion obfervable among them in point of age and fize, and the diffimilarity of their drefs, which was alfo dirty and ragged, fet off the French to great advantage, who, notwithftanding fo much fatigue, maintained at all times an erect, foldierly and vigorous air. But we were all furprifed at the good condition of the Englifh troops, as well as their cleanlinefs of drefs; to account for their good appearance, Cornwallis had opened all the ftores to the foldiers before the capitulation took place. Each had on a complete new fuit, but all their finery feemed only to humble them the more when contrafted with the miferable appearance of the Americans; thefe haughty Englifhmen did not even dare to look up at their conquerors; filent and afhamed they one after an other depofited their arms in the ftipulated place, and that they might not fink and die under their humiliation, we kept the fpectators at a confiderable diftance. Upon their return, the Englifh officers had the civility to pay a compliment to the meaneft of the French, which they did not deign to do to the Americans of the higheft rank. §   This

§ *An officer belonging to the American army remarked, that after the furrender, the Englifh behaved with the fame overbearing infolence as if they had been conquerors, the Scots wept bitterly, while the Germans only conducted themfelves decently, and in a manner becoming Prifoners.—With a meannefs always attendant upon vanquifhed infolence, the Englifh fervilely cringed to the French, vainly attempting to fcreen the difgrace of being conquered by thofe they had fo often denominated American rebels, and republicans.*

This hatred betwixt the two nations has manifested itself upon several occasions; and such of the English as remained disarmed at York, had to bear a great deal from the Americans, who seemed resolved to take ample vengeance for the robberies and murders that had been perpetrated in their habitations. Among others I saw the lady of an English Colonel come to our camp, with tears in her eyes, to beg the protection of a French guard to defend her and her infants from the violence of an American soldier. The next day after the surrender, the officers that were prisoners came over to view our entrenchments, but when they went to examine those of the Americans, they were driven away with contempt and indignation. During the whole time they remained at York, I do not remember that they had the least connexion or intercourse with the Americans, while they lived upon familiar terms with the French, and sought upon all occasions to give them proofs of their esteem. ‡

I have been through the unfortunate little town of York since the siege, and saw many elegant houses shot through and through in a thousand places, and ready to crumble to pieces; rich household furniture crushed under their ruins, or broken by the brutal English soldier; carcases of men and horses, half covered with dirt, whose mouldering limbs, while they poisoned the air, struck dread and horror to the soul: Books piled in heaps, and scattered among the ruins of the buildings, served to give me an idea of the taste and morals of the inhabitants; these were either treatises of religion or controversial divinity; the *history* of the English nation, and their foreign settlements; *collections* of *charters* and *acts* of parliaments; the works of the celebrated *Alexander Pope*; a translation of *Montaigne's Essays*; *Gil Blas de Santillane*, and the excellent *Essay upon Women*, § by *Mr. Thomas.*

The plan of the fortifications for the defence of York and Glocester, has been entirely changed; they are drawing them into a narrower compass than before, have destroyed the English works, and are busy at constructing new ones. The travelling artillery is partly at Williamsburg and partly at York; and the heavy cannon is at West point (called *Delaware* in the maps,) a place situated between the two rivers that form that of York.

On the twenty-fourth, the troops began to go into winter quarters. The regiments of Bourbonnais and Royal Deux Ponts are

I

‡ *The English newspapers have given the French full credit for the generosity and delicacy with which they treated the British prisoners. It has been observed that the English, when conquered, always praise the generosity of their French conquerors.—Have the English, when victorious, ever given the conquered Frenchman the same reason for grateful acknowledgement?*

§ *There is hardly a place in America, where I have been, that I have not met with this work.*

are at Williamſburg, where our head Quarters are fixed. The regiment of Soiſſonnais, and the grenadier companies, and Chaſſeurs of Saintonge are at York. The reſt of the regiment of Saintonge is billeted about in the country betwixt York and Hampton ; and this latter place, ſituated on James River, is occupied by the Legion of Lauzun.   I am, &c.

LETTER XII.   *Character of General Burgoyne.—Account of his unfortunate expedition in* 1777 *——Magnanimity of ſir Guy Carleton.— A conſiderable body of Indians join Burgoyne—He makes a ſpeech to them.—Ticonderoga abandoned by the Americans. The Surrender of General Burgoyne and his army at Saratoga.— A compariſon betwixt General Burgoyne and Lord Cornwallis.*

York, November 14, 17⁸1.

THE American war, the ſucceſs of which has appeared ſo dubious, offers to our view two events, almoſt unparalleled in any war that hiſtory has recorded in her annals : I mean two entire armies made priſoners, who neverthelefs were under the direction of Generals of the firſt note and ability. It now remains to aſk, which of the two has diſcovered the deepeſt talents, and the moſt activity, or experienced the greateſt obſtacles, and committed the moſt miſtakes.

Being myſelf a witneſs to the efforts of one army, and ſurrounded by perſons who had a ſhare in reducing the other, having alſo in my hands ſome exact and faithful accounts of that affair, I will venture a few reflections.

Let us in the firſt place take a curſory view of Burgoyne's campaign, and we ſhall be the better enabled to compare him with his brother in misfortune, *Lord Cornwallis.*

Burgoyne, formed by nature with an active, enterpriſing diſpoſition, animated by a moſt extravagant love of glory, a favorite alſo of the court of London, was furniſhed amply with the means of ſecuring the moſt brilliant ſucceſs. His army conſiſted of ſeven thouſand one hundred and ſeventy three regular troops, Engliſh and Germans, excluſive of a corps of artillery, and ſeven or eight hundred men, under the orders of Colonel St. Leger : all his officers were men of approved merit, and he was provided with a conſiderable train of artillery and ammunition of every ſort. Guy Carleton, Governor of Canada, who had the care of furniſhing the particular articles, forgot nothing that might contribute to the ſucceſs of the expedition. The ſervices this governor had rendered to the crown,—the preſervation of Canada, which was owing to his exertions alone, and the perfect knowledge he had of the whole country, ſeem to have given him the beſt pretenſions to the
chief

chief command, but he had a spirit great enough to forget this piece of injustice ;* and went so far in favour of his rival, as to consent to make treaties with the savages, tho' contrary to his own private opinion, and from them obtained a considerable body of Indians and warriors. The unsteady, capricious temper of these people, their barbarous and bloody customs, their thirst for plunder, their infidelity in fulfilling their engagements, did not all hinder the English from making them the companions of their expected conquests: Burgoyne harangued them with an eloquent oration on the shores of Lake Champlaine, calculated to inflame their courage and restrain their barbarity. But what influence can eloquence have over the minds of those men, who in their whole language have not two words to signify *equity* and *humanity.*†

The

* *They have now made him their commander in chief in North-America, in the room of Sir Henry Clinton. Misfortunes are necessary in every country to silence cabal and intrigue, and render impartial justice to merit ; but it too often happens, that applications to really deserving men come too late to be of any service.*

† *These Savages being parceiled out into numerous tribes, have consequently manners more or less barbarous ; several of them take the membrane that covers the scull, from the enemies they kill in battle, and carry it off in triumph, with the hair on, and even drink their blood.*
The Spaniards have been reproached for exercising cruelties upon the inhabitants of the countries they conquered ; but it appears that reproaches of this kind are no less well founded against the English.
An Indian speech that was given me by a professor at Williamsburg, a translation of which is subjoined, is a proof of this. It discovers at the same time, the bold and masculine energy with which these savages are taught by nature to express themselves.
Speech of the Savage LONAN, *in a General Assembly, as it was sent to the Governor of Virginia ; anno* 1754.
" LONAN *will no longer oppose making the proposed peace with*
" *the white men—you are sensible that he never knew what fear is—*
" *that he never turned his back in the day of battle—no one has more*
" *love for the white men than I have. The war we have had with*
" *them, has been long, and bloody on both sides—rivers of blood have*
" *ran on all parts, and yet no good has resulted therefrom to any—I*
" *once more repeat it—let us be at peace with these men ; I will for-*
" *get our injuries, the interest of my country demands it—I will for-*
" *get—but difficult indeed is the task—yes—I will forget—that Ma-*
" *jor Rogers cruelly and inhumanly murdered, in their canoes, my*
" *wife, my children, my father, my mother, and all my kindred.—*
" *This roused me to deeds of vengeance !—I was cruel in despight of*
" *myself—I will die content if my country is once more at peace ; but*
" *when Lonan shall be no more, who, alas, will drop a tear to the*
" *memory of Lonan !*"

The firſt attempts of Burgoyne before Ticonderoga, were crowned with the moſt flattering ſuccefs. This place, built by the French, in 1756, is ſituated weſtward, towards the ſtreight that preſerves the communication between the Lakes *George*, and *Champlaine*, upon a point of land covered with ſharp rocks, and hemmed in by water on three ſides. The part adjoining the main land is covered by a deep marſh, and defended by the old French lines : to theſe the Americans had added ſeveral other works, and a group of fortifications, called by them a *block-houſe*. They alſo fortified the ſummit and the foot of a high mountain, on the eaſtern ſide, called *Mount Independence*, and with aſtoniſhing ardour and induſtry united both theſe poſts, by a bridge thown over the ſtreight, ſupported by twenty-two huge piles, each fifty feet long and twelve thick, faſtened together by cramp irons and large chains.

Lake Champlaine was, on the ſide next the bridge, defended by a boom, compoſed of beams laſhed together, and wound round with chains. By this means a communication was not only kept up between the two poſts, but no poſſibility of accefs offered on the northern ſide.

Although Ticonderoga is of itſelf lofty, it is nevertheleſs commanded, in eminence, by another mountain called *Sugar Hill*, from its being in the form of a ſugar loaf. The Americans had entertained thoughts of fortifying it, but concluded that the works were already too extenſive for their means of defence, and expected that its difficulty of accefs, and the rocky inequality of its ſurface would hinder the enemy from taking advantage of its ſituation.

The royal army advanced with great caution along the ſides of the lake, having in the center their fleet, which, on its coming up, anchored within cannon ſhot of the enemy. On the approach of the right wing, the Americans, to the great ſurpriſe of the royaliſts, abandoned their works on the ſide next Lake George, and ſet fire to them: Major General Philips then took poſſeſſion of an advantageous poſt on Mount *Hope*, which, beſides that it commanded their lines, cut off their communication with the lake. It is ſaid the Americans ſhewed but little courage in defending the other poſts on this ſide as well as on the other.

The Britiſh army advanced with an equal celerity on the other ſide of the lake, and in a ſhort time inveſted all their works. The advantages that Sugar Hill preſented, ſoon determined the Engliſh to build redoubts there, and the paths they were obliged to climb, upon a rugged and almoſt perpendicular ſurface, did not hinder the alert Major General Philips from erecting his works in a very ſhort ſpace of time.

The American Generals now thought proper to hold a council of war, in which was repreſented, " that they had not above half the neceſſary number of working hands, that the neceſſity for labour increaſed as the hands diminiſhed, and that the place would be inevitably and completely inveſted in leſs than twenty-four hours.''

hours." It was then unanimously refolved to evacuate the poft, which was immediately put in execution.

It has been fince afked, with a degree of reproach, " why, if the forces were not fufficient to defend it, did they not withdraw the troops; remove the artillery and ftores and demolifh the fortifications before the arrival of the enemy? Why did they wait to be furrounded, at an inftant when a retreat was apparently more prejudicial than a furrender upon fuch terms as might have been granted, and which would have been infinitely preferable to the rifque they ran of having their fortifications carried by affault?"

Immediately, upon the determination of the council to evacuate the place, the American army embarked their baggage, their artillery, and their provifions in a decked veffel, and more than two hundred batteaus, efcorted by five gallies; directing their courfe towards Skenefborough, while the garrifon marched towards Cafiletown.

The next morning the royalifts having difcovered the precipitate flight of the Americans, took poffeffion of the bridge and fortifications, and this enormous mafs, which had coft more than twenty months labour, was now cut up in lefs time than it would take to relate it. By five in the morning, the frigates *Royal George*, and *Inflexible* * had a free paffage through, and Burgoyne loft no time in purfuing the enemy by water, whilft the troops marched after them by land. He overtook them, at length, near *Skenefborough falls*, where he feized two of the gallies, and blew up three others. The Americans, being now in a defperate fituation, fet fire to their batteaus, mills and fortifications, and faved themfelves in the woods, unprovided, and deftitute of every thing.

Confufion and difmay predominated in like manner among the forces on the left; the foldiers no longer obeyed the commands of their officers, and in this fituation Brigadier General Frazer came up with their rear guard, with a body of troops far inferior, and attacked them, expecting every moment to be joined by General Reidfel. The Americans, at firft defended themfelves bravely, but at the coming up of the laft mentioned commander, they fled precipitately, after lofing a confiderable number of their men, together with Colonel Francis, their leader, and one of their braveft officers. General Saint-Clair, who commanded the van guard, when informed of thefe difaftrous circumftances, took immediately to the woods, in doubt whether to march to the upper parts of Connecticut or towards Fort Edward. Colonel Hill was detached from Skenefborough, with the ninth regiment towards Fort Anne, and on his way, fell in, with a body of American troops, fix times as numerous as his own, which he defeated after three hours engaging, The Americans then burnt Fort Anne, and fled to Fort Edward upon Hudfon's river.

General

* *This fhip was built in twenty eight days and mounted eighteen twelve pounders.*

General Saint-Clair arrived at Fort Edward, (where General Schuyler commanded,) with the remains of his army, after a march of seven days, in a moft deplorable condition, having fuffered every diftrefs that imagination can conceive, from the bad quality of the water, and want of cloaths and provifions : He was here joined by the other fugitives, equally weak, fatigued and difcouraged.

Burgoyne, without lofing time, fet out from Skenefborough, on his march to Fort Edward, but encountered great difficulties and embarraffments, although the diftance is not very confiderable ; for the country is naturally fo wild, fo defert, fo incumbered with marfhes, interfected with creeks, and the enemy had fo increafed thefe natural obftacles by huge lines of abbatis, that it is not eafy to conceive how much he had to fuffer in furmounting thefe difficulties. He had to conftruct near forty bridges or caufeways, and one of them, made of trunks of trees, was more than a mile in length. It is true, he might have avoided all this trouble in taking his rout round by Ticonderoga, but he feared a retrograde movement of his army might give the Americans time to recover their courage, and flacken the ardour of his own troops.

It is worth while to obferve, that in all this diftrefs, misfortune, and univerfal confternation, not a fingle diftrict in America feemed in the leaft difpofed to come in, or make its fubmiffion. The danger did not difcourage even thofe States which were moft expofed to the depredations of the enemy ; under the direction of the Congrefs they all united with the greateft vigour to repulfe them ; and General Arnold was difpatched to the Northern army with a train of artillery, furnifhed him by General Wafhington on purpofe for this expedition. At his arrival, he ordered the troops from Saratoga to a place called *Stillwater*, in order to be in a better fituation to check the progrefs of Colonel Saint Leger, who was advancing toward the Mohawk river. His troops, however, (St. Leger's) fuffered great loffes from the Indians : the efforts of Burgoyne not being fufficient to reftrain their cruelty, friends as well as enemies fell alike victims to their thirft of blood. The murder of Mifs *M'Crea*, in particular, ftruck terror into every heart: She was then in the bloom and innocence of beauty and youth, her father was attached to the royal party, and upon the very day that fhe fell a facrifice to the wanton barbarity of the favages, fhe was to have been married to an Englifh officer.

Scenes fo fhocking as thefe, irritated the people almoft to diftraction, and kindled a fpirit of hatred, even in the difaffected, againft a government capable of accepting *allies*, more difpofed to extirpate than fubdue the people, whom they claimed as fubjects.

The Americans now began to think it their duty to defend not only the rights of their country, but alfo thofe that nature herfelf had given them. Each citizen became a foldier, and when their regular forces feemed almoft annihilated, defpair poured forth multitudes, ftill more formidable, from the woods, the mountains, and the borders of the marfhes.

It

It was now that Burgoyne's army began to experience real difficulties, in the neighbourhood of Fort Edward ; —in proportion as
they advanced, obstacles multiplied on every side; for fifteen
days, they were employed in bringing down batteaus and provisions
from Fort George to Hudson's river, a distance of more than eighteen miles : this excessive labour was quite unequal to the waste of
time and provisions ; they did not receive one third of the horses
they expected from Canada, on account of the length of the way,
and the great number of water passages; and for the same reason
they could not collect more than fifty pair of oxen ; heavy rains
added still more to their difficulties, and in the end, they found it
impossible to establish magazines to continue their operations.

Intelligence was at last received, that Colonel Saint Leger had
arrived before, and was directing his views against, Fort Stanwix :
Burgoyne upon this, concluded, with some reason, that if he could
prosecute his march rapidly forward, and advance down the Mohawk river, supposing at the same time Colonel Saint Leger to
succeed in his attack on the fort, he should draw the enemy between two fires, or at least have it in his power to force them to
change their situation, and retreat to a greater distance, which
would consequently open the Mohawk country to him, and afford
him the means of executing his intended junction.

However just this plan might be, it could not be carried into
execution for want of provisions, to connect so long a chain of posts
with Fort George ; and because the enemy had a body of troops at
White-Creek, sufficient to break it.

He abandoned this project then, and fell upon a scheme of surprising Bennington, where the Americans had great stores of corn
and cattle. Bennington lies between two branches of the river
Hoosick, about twenty miles east of the Hudson, a place of little
importance, and incapable by its situation of ever becoming considerable, unless some remarkable changes should take place.
This expedition Burgoyne intrusted to Colonel Baum, a German,
and gave him five hundred men, and two pieces of artillery for the
purpose ; and to be the better enabled to make the best of such advantages as should be gained, he fixed his main camp before Saratoga, and made a bridge of boats over the river, upon which the
advanced corps might pass. During these transactions, the corps
of Colonel Breyman, consisting of light infantry, was posted at
Battenkill, with a design, if necessary, to support Colonel Baum.
The latter, in his march, fell in with a small provision convoy
of the enemy, which he took : But the want of waggons and
horses, made his march so long and fatiguing, that the Americans
got intelligence of his design, and had time to prepare to receive
him. The Colonel, upon his approach to the place, finding that
his force was not sufficient to make an attack, with a prospect of
success, posted himself in as favourable a situation as possible, and
sent off an express to the General. Breyman then had orders to
reinforce Colonel Baum, without loss of time : He obeyed, but
his

his march was long and difficult, meeting with nothing but bad water and bad roads ; the want of horfes and wheel carriages, added ftill more to his embarraffments, and a long continuance of heavy rains, rendered his condition almoft as wretched as can poffibly be conceived. But the American General, Starke, who commanded the Bennington militia, effectually prevented their junction. He marched on the 16th of Auguft to attack Colonel Baum, and the latter was fo far from expecting fuch a vifit, that he took him at firft for the reinforcement he was waiting for : However, he made a very brave defence, but his little works were foon forced on all fides ; the Indians and the Englifh provincial troop⁵, had already ran away into the woods, and there remained only the Germans, who, after they had expended all their powder, charged the enemy fword in hand, but were finally forced to furrender prifoners of war, after feeing their Colonel fall.

A little after this action arrives Colonel Breyman, without knowing any thing of what had paffed : Inftead of friends, he faw himfelf fuddenly furrounded by American forces ; but the fatigued and exhaufted ftate of his troops did not prevent him from making a foldierly defence. He even drove the enemy from two or three heights ; but was, however, at laft overpowered by numbers ; and after firing away all his ammunition, made a retreat with great difficulty, leaving two pieces of artillery in the hands of the enemy. Their lofs in thefe two actions, amounted in killed, wounded and miffing to five or fix hundred men ; and in this ftroke, Fortune now, for the firft time, fince the death of General Montgomery, fhowed herfelf favourable to the Americans in their expeditions to the north: The militia at length found they *could* conquer regular forces ; an opinion of more confequence at this time than the gaining of a great battle upon other occafions.

While Saint Leger was employed, with various fuccefs in befieging Fort Stanwix, General Harkimer came at the head of nine hundred of the militia of the country to relieve and victual the fort : Upon this Saint Leger, fearing an attack in his entrenchments, fixed an ambufcade, compofed of regulars and Indians to intercept them. The militia, a thing almoft incredible in a country where this kind of warfare is ufual, fell blindly into it, loft a confiderable number, and could not be rallied but with the greateft difficulty. The Governor of the fort, Colonel Ganfevoort, informed, in the mean time, of what had happened, haftened to make a diverfion in favour of his friends, penetrated into the Englifh camp, plundered it, carried off a great quantity of fuch articles as he was in want of, and made fome prifoners. §

Colonel Saint Leger, after his fuccefs, neglected nothing to engage the befieged to furrender. The Governor, however, continued deaf to his menaces, as well as to his promifes and intreaties.

In

§ Note, *this fally was made under the immediate direction of Colonel Willet.*

In the skirmish with the militia, the Indians did not get the booty they expected ; they besides lost several of their warriors, celebrated among them for their bravery, and now learnt with extreme vexation that General Arnold was coming to the relief of the place with a thousand men, and that Burgoyne had met with several checks, if not totally ruined. Their discontent and ill humour was then carried to excess : notwithstanding all that could be said or done to calm, and retain these dastards with the army, they left the camp, after having robbed the officers, pillaged the stores, cut the throats of several of the soldiers and stolen their arms and provisions, which in the end forced Colonel Saint Leger to raise the siege in haste, and even leave behind a part of his baggage. This last piece of news completed the joy and confidence of the Americans, while Gansevoort and Willet, who had defended the place, were ranked, as well as General Starke and Colonel Warner, in the number of the Saviours of their country.

Burgoyne, supplying himself constantly with provisions from Fort George, but with great difficulty, passed Hudson's River about the middle of September, the enemy being at that time in the vicinity of Stillwater. The Ministry and Parliament have examined whether this march was either necessary or seasonable, but it has not appeared that any sufficient arguments have been brought against it : it is evident, that Burgoyne was determined in his measures not only by immediate circumstances, but also by the instructions of his court. He afterwards advanced through bye-roads and routs little frequented, along the river, on the same side with the enemy, and often separated from them only by thin woods. He marched in person at the head of the English line, which formed the right wing. This wing was covered by General Frazer, and Colonel Breyman, with the grenadiers and light infantry, Indian escorts, Provincials and Canadians : the left wing and the artillery, commanded by Majors Philips, and Reidsel, followed the shores of the river.

The Americans now presented themselves in force to attack the flank of the English line. The latter were not a little surprised, when they saw with what boldness the enemy began the attack, and with what vigour and obstinacy they supported it from three in the afternoon till sun-set. General Arnold led on his troops, and courted danger with an ardor and intrepidity, which although natural to his character, could never have been shown to better advantage : the Americans however were constantly reinforced with fresh troops, whilst, on the side of the English, the weight and burden of the action was almost continually sustained by the same persons.

Major-General Philips, upon hearing the first fire, marched with a part of the artillery across a piece of woods, very difficult of access, and his arrival, in a critical minute, for that time saved the army, who remained masters of the field. This victory was honourably gained, but gave them to know, that the Americans

K   were

were capable of defending themselves, not only in entrenchments, and behind walls and hedges, but in the open field, uncovered, and for a considerable space of time. The English remained under arms the whole night, and at day-break advanced within cannon shot of the enemy, fortifying their wings and extending their left towards the river ; but they found the Americans too much upon their guard to be meddled with.

The fatigues the army had undergone, and the discouraging prospect they had before them, confounded at once all the hopes and expectations with which the Indians, in particular, had flattered themselves ; it was now impossible to get any further services from them; they became sullen and intractable, and upon the General finding some fault with their conduct, they abandoned the army and went off in a pet, at a time when it stood most in need of their assistance. This Indian desertion brought on others among the English, as well as the Provincial and Canadian troops.

Burgoyne had still however, some hopes of being succoured by an army from New-York ; with much difficulty he received a letter from Sir Henry Clinton in cyphers, informing him that he was about to make a diversion in his favour upon the North river, by attacking Fort Montgomery and several other of the neighbouring fortresses : Burgoyne by way of answer, pressed him for assistance, gave an account of his situation, and informed him that his provisions could not hold out longer than the twelfth of the ensuing month.

The army under the command of General Gates, increasing from day to day, obliged Burgoyne to fortify with the greatest attention, and to add considerably to the number of guards, which necessarily increased the fatigue and weakened the troops : the late successes of the militia had likewise made them more enterprising than before, and those of New-Hampshire and the upper parts of Connecticut, commanded by General Lincoln, recovered Ticonderoga and Mount Independence, made themselves masters of lake George, and thus cut off Burgoyne from all communication with Canada.

In the beginning of October this unfortunate General was obliged to diminish his rations, and then determined, whatever might be the consequence, to force himself a passage through the country. For this purpose he picked out the choicest of his troops, and the bravest and best experienced of his officers : but the Americans perceiving his design, came down by thousands to attack him. It was then that the English began to sink under the numbers of their enemies; they were forced to retire within their lines, into which General Arnold pursued them with his usual impetuosity, and would infallibly have forced them, had he not received a wound.

Colonel Breyman, who commanded a German corps de reserve, was still more unfortunate ; his camp was attacked and carried,

his

his baggage pillaged, his cannon taken, and he himself perished in the action. This day the English lost a part of their bravest men, and nothing could exceed their misery and distress ; they laboured the whole night to change their position, hoping to oblige the enemy to change theirs also. This business was accomplished with incredible silence and activity, and in the morning they offered battle to the Americans, who declined it ; considering, with good reason, that it would be better to fatigue and harrass a brave and desperate enemy, than to expose themselves to the chance of a decisive action.

The English General was now informed, that the enemy had dispatched forward a considerable body, to surround him entirely. This, he took every measure in his power to prevent, and upon the night of the ninth of October, began to march, leaving his sick and wounded to provide for themselves ; but the care General Gates took of these has been since gratefully acknowledged by the English themselves.

A heavy rain, that lasted the whole night, rendered their progress very slow ; and at break of day he perceived the Americans posted and fortified on the heights around him. He then took a resolution to march towards Fort Edward, but his road cutters being repulsed, and the opposite shore of the river lined with enemies, he concluded to call a council of war ; upon considering the matter, they saw no other probable way of reaching this Fort than by a night march, and the soldiers carrying their provisions on their backs : But while they were preparing to execute this forlorn purpose, they learnt that the enemy had taken sufficient precautions to prevent the execution of their design.

Nothing could have been more wretched—nothing more deplorable than the condition of this army. Worn down by a long series of severe duty, marches and actions ; forsaken by the Indians in the needful moment, weakened by desertion, dejected and discouraged by the timidity of the Canadians and provincial troops, their regular corps reduced by repeated losses, to the number of only three thousand five hundred, their bravest officers killed, the rest forced to be continually under arms, harrassed day and night, by an enemy that seemed to grow out of the ground on every side, having lost all hope of relief, and but three days provisions left, their last resource was to make the best terms they could with the enemy. The General, willing however, in an affair that regarded the future well-being of every individual in the army, to have their unanimous voice, as far as possible, called a council of war, inviting not only the generals and staff officers, but all the commanding captains : these universally gave it as their opinion, *that the army could not do otherwise than treat with General Gates*; and the English have since done the latter the justice to declare, that, considering the ground on which he stood, he showed not the least mark of insolence or arrogance.——

The

The fubftance of the principal articles was, that the army fhould march out of their camp with the honours of war, and their artillery, to an appointed place, where they fhould pile their arms : that a paffage fhould be granted them from Bofton to Europe, upon condition of their net ferving in America during the prefent war.————They reckoned their lofs from the fixth of July, to the capitulation, inclufive, to amount to near ten thoufand men.

The great fault of Burgoyne, and what prepared the way to all his misfortunes, was his march to Fort Edward; if he had returned to Ticonderoga, and proceeded to Fort George, he would doubtlefs have avoided thefe difafters, but, as has been obferved, he feared that a retrograde movement would flacken the ardour of his troops, and give the Americans time to recover from their furprife. A General is always blameable when he ventures far into unexplored countries; but Burgoyne, who had feen the Americans fly, on all fides, at his approach, notwithftanding their fuperiority in number, and thofe vaft fortifications which both nature and art had rendered impregnable, could he believe that thefe very men would afterwards dare to fhow themfelves, furround him on every fide, and fight him in the open field ?

The fhame of re-iterated defeats, the immediate calamities they felt, and greater ftill to be expected, the dread of Indian cruelty and indifcriminate plunder; all thefe confiderations muft have wrought wonderfully on the minds of the Americans to have produced fo fudden and univerfal a change; let it be remembered, however, that the very elements affifted in the reduction of Burgoyne; the heavy rains threw continual obftacles in his way, particularly in the affair of Bennington, where, by delaying the march of Colonel Breyman, General Starke had an opportunity of attacking and defeating Colonel Baum, before the other's arrival; the Indians, likewife, forfook him at the very time when they could be of ufe to him; his expected reinforcements never joined him; and Clinton, who then commanded at New-York, and might with the greateft eafe have failed in force up the North River, was too flow in making the diverfion. All that genius, activity and courage could fuggeft was put into practice by Burgoyne; his marches were judicious, his pofitions advantageous, and his fkirmifhes obftinate: But the Americans, reanimated by hope, and emboldened by defpair, became every day more numerous active and warlike.

As to Lord Cornwallis, he had to contend with enemies better difciplined and longer inured to war, but he had the advantage of Burgoyne in long experience in America, in a more exact knowledge of the country, in being better fupplyed with provifions and ammunition and not having to ftruggle with fuch fevere weather and impaffable tracts of wildernefs: He had alfo the moft perfect confidence of his troops and was become fo formidable to the enemy, that General Wafhington was thought to be the only man that could, as fuch, be placed in competition with him. Burgoyne had conftantly to do with enemies who were either ftrongly en-

trenched or infinitely more numerous than his own troops. Cornwallis, on the contrary, at the head of an army of at leaft eight
thoufand choice troops, and always fuperior to his difperfed
enemies, yet, ftrange as it may feem, did not think proper to attack
the Marquis de la Fayette, who never had more at any time than
two thoufand, nor to hinder the landing of three thoufand men under
the orders of M. de Saint Simon, to prevent them from joining the
Marquis. If he had marched down upon them at their firft landing he would have found a body of men totally ignorant of the
country they were in, their arms and ammunition yet on board the
veffels, and not a fingle intrenchment thrown up: fuperior to them
ftill, after their junction with the Marquis, and threatened with
the approach of the armies of General Wafhington and Count
Rochambeau, ought he not to have haftened, by forced marches,
to attack and difperfe them, that he might afterwards have it in his
power to make head againft the others?

But if, after the inftructions of Clinton, and his promifes of
fpeedily relieving him, he neverthelefs thought it improper to
hazard any attack, how advantageous foever it might promife to
be, he ought at leaft to have done all in his power to retard and
prolong the fiege; for whatever might have been the relief promifed
by Clinton, contrary winds might have delayed its arrival, and a
few days gained would have been of the greateft importance to
him. He likewife knew that Count de Graffe had declared that
he could not remain but a fhort time in the bay; fo that, retarding
his departure, would have been deranging his plans, and confequently hindering him from ferving his country elfewhere: The
feafon being, alfo, pretty well advanced, the autumnal rains
muft have made the fiege very fatiguing to our troops, and perhaps
have occafioned contagious diftempers among them, in a country where the air and water are lefs wholefome than more north-
ward. †

The diftance between York and Williamfburg is twelve miles,
and this whole interval is covered with very thick woods; it would
certainly have been an eafy matter then, for Cornwallis to have
made lines of *abbatis* throughout this foreft, and have ftopped up
the

---

* It was believed, at firft, that Cornwallis's army did not confift
of more than four or five thoufand men: without this prefumption it
would have been highly imprudent in M. de Saint Simon to have
landed his troops, before the arrival of General Wafhington and Count
Rochambeau. But if notwithftanding that, their landing had been
attended with ill confequences, he would certainly have been liable to
fevere reprehenfion.

† This is the more probable, as the lines being very extenfive, in
refpect to the number of men, the duty was more conftant. Some foldiers
were eleven nights without lying down in their tents, a greater number feven or eight, and the reft four or five.

the roads from poſt to poſt; three thouſand ſlaves at leaſt, which he had taken from the planters, would have rendered this mode of defence ſtill more practicable——all our military connoiſſeurs have given it as their opinion that a few detachmens and ſome field pieces, might have retarded the combined army at leaſt a month in its approaches to the works at York, and probably would have deſtroyed us a great number of men. The lands adjoining the town were covered with Indian corn, and by taking it away or burning it, he would have obliged the aſſailants to get food for their horſes at a greater diſtance, and by that means delayed the tranſportation of the artillery, which was landed ſeveral miles from the camp.

Cornwallis thus ſhut up in York, with artillery badly enough ſerved, and his works diſadvantageouſly conſtructed, had it not in his power to ſally out upon us without riſquing too much, while the beſiegers had time to prepare to receive him, and even to cut off his retreat : being thus incapacitated from acting offenſively, he could no way extricate himſelf but by ſome deſperate attempt.

If he had known how to profit by circumſtances, the relief promiſed by Clinton might have ſaved him, or at leaſt made a great diverſion in his favour. The Engliſh ſquadron, conſiſting of twenty-ſeven or twenty-eight ſhips of the line, with four thouſand land forces on board, appeared before the capes on the 26th of October, that is to ſay, ſeven days after the ſurrender. Count de Graſſe's fleet, being thirty-ſix ſhips of the line, was then at anchor within the *Horſe-Shoe,* a ſand bank, over which veſſels of war cannot paſs, except through a narrow channel on the eaſt ſide ; the wind blowing at that time right in, compleatly prevented the ſquadron from getting under way, and conſequently could not have hindered Clinton from effecting a landing for his troops. I cannot ſay whether it was a fear of bad weather that inclined the Count to make choice of this place, but his over great precaution was, I am ſure, an obſtacle to his purſuit of the Engliſh, the wind being favourable enough, had the fleet been in any other place.

May we now aſk which of the two Engliſh Generals has manifeſted the beſt conduct ? For my part I am of opinion, Burgoyne would have ſucceeded better in defending York, and that Cornwallis * could not have done more in the wilderneſs, adjacent to Saratoga.   I am, &c.

LETTER

* *And yet Cornwallis has received univerſal applauſe in England, while Burgoyne experienced nothing but ſatire, contempt and invective. Reputations are like fortunes, they may be acquired by the baſeſt means. Cornwallis's reception upon his arrival in England, was undoubtedly favourable beyond his warmeſt hopes ; but the following anecdote will give us ſome idea what his expectations were, when he left Virginia.*

Soon after the ſurrender, as General Waſhington and Cornwallis were walking together, the General obſerving his hat under his arm, re-

LETTER XIII. *Advantages arising to America, from the capture of Lord Cornwallis.—The future importance of this country—Her various local advantages over Europe—Political happiness arising from the abolishment of the feudal system of laws in America—The free and independent situation of the American peasantry—National character of the people in America, not yet arrived to maturity—Their natural ingenuity and inventive turn—The political conduct of the English Ministry, respecting America, previous to the breaking out of the war—Proceedings of the first American Congress——General Gage and the Boston port bill—The American alliance with France—Reflexions arising therefrom— A long peace in America, after the war— Religion will probably be the first cause of dissension in the United States— A unity of faith and worship, most likely to render mankind happy in every part of the world.*

York, November 15, 1781.

THIS great and happy event, in which the French have had so considerable a share, will soon give a new turn to American affairs. The southern states so long harrassed and distrest, will now assume new spirit and activity. The power of Congress, heretofore weak and wavering, will be consolidated, and the prejudices against our nation will vanish. To what a pitch of grandeur will not these new states shortly arise!

Extending more than six hundred leagues from north to south, and much more from east to west, situated in temperate and serene climates, where the variety of latitudes, and the natural fertility of the soil, will soon supply them with all those productions, which other nations cannot procure without traversing immense seas and oceans, what advantages will they not enjoy!

This country is intersected and watered in every part, with lakes, rivers, creeks and rivulets. The lakes, and some of the rivers open a communication with very distant regions, a conveniency which cannot be enjoyed in other parts of the world to any great perfection, without the previous assistance of art, and the toil and labour of men in digging canals. There are also rich mines concealed in the bowels of the earth, especially that most useful of all metals, iron; and the sea coast, through which so many great rivers

quested his Lordship to be covered—he declined it; upon which his Excellency continued his request, adding at the same time, " your head, my Lord, will be apt to catch cold."— Sir, replied his Lordship, (at the same time striking his head three times with his hand) as to my head, it is no matter what becomes of it now!

vers difcharge their waters, is every where indented with bays, ha-
vens, roads, and ports, which abound with fifh of the moft excellent kinds. The Banks of Newfoundland will always be a
nurfery for feamen, while the forefts and the plains will continue
to produce wood, tar and hemp, for the conftructing and rigging
of fhips.

Our European cities and towns, for the moft part, afford us to
this day ftriking proofs of the calamities, ignorance, mifery and
barbarity of our anceftors, in their unpleafant, unhealthy fituati-
ons, in their walls planted round with battlements, their formidable turrets of defence, their clofe and compact buildings, almoft
without air or light, and their crooked, muddy ftreets, equally
incommodious and difgufting; but the American towns are upon
a different plan; not walled in, as if mankind were to live in
eternal diftruft of each other, they are built on agreeable falubrious
fpots of land, wafhed by pure and navigable waters, furrounded
by fertile fields, laid out in fpacious ftreets croffing each other in
direct lines, and ornamented with buildings every where beautiful
convenient and regular.

If America, in point of foil, bids fair to exceed Europe, what
will fhe not do in her legiflation and her manners?

Our medley of cuftoms at once abfurd, unjuft and contradictory,
the barbarous, complicated fyftems of feudal laws, ancient legiflation and modern manners, will never be united here under one and
the fame government, will never take up the whole time and abilities of men of genius to unravel their meaning, or require numerous
tribunals to difcufs them; or become a mere labyrinth wherein the
fubtil orator may hide himfelf, or furprife his adverfary; and
under the fanction of which the all grafping lawyer may rob the
widow and the orphan of their rights. * Here, the criminal in
irons will dare to raife his voice, and call his defenders to his
aid; and the laws, averfe to fanguinary meafures, will patiently
attend to all he has to fay, before it pronounces fentence againft
him.

Barbarous prejudices will not arm citizen againft citizen, friend
againft friend, expofe the oppreffed to be crufhed by the oppreffor,
or banifh from their country its moft ufeful defenders; feparate
fathers from their families, wives from their hufbands, children
from their parents; and produce thofe fhameful abfurdities which
                                                            lay

---

* *I would not be underftood to fay, that the civil legiflation in the
United States of America is actually exempt from all thefe inconve-
niencies and abufes: formed upon that of England, at leaft as
defective as ours, and framed in the midft of the troubles of a revolution, they may mend and correct their conftitutions, but never while
their troubles laft, bring them to perfection. It is in the calms of
peace that ftudious men, enlightened by experience, will be enabled to
free them from confufion, and of whatever is unfuitable to their climate
and cuftoms.*

lay the foldier under the wretched neceffity either of violating the laws of humanity, of religion, of his country—or to lofe at once the fruit of his fervices and dangers, and appear no longer among his countrymen except with difgrace and infamy. ‡ Legions

‡ *In a difpute betwixt a French and an American officer (the only one that has happened) the Frenchman firft drew his fword; the American refufed to follow his example and finding his long halbert a more certain weapon of defence, wounded his adverfary therewith. In France he would have been driven with difgrace out of the army, but General Washington contented himfelf with punifhing the American, not for having combated with unequal arms, but for raifing a difturbance in the army.*

The practice of duelling deprives us of feveral thoufand men yearly; a lofs the more confiderable, as they are for the moft part experienced officers, accuftomed to difcipline and able to bear fatigue, but whofe places are often fupplied by raw young fellows, ruined by debauchery, and moft of whom fink under the weight of the fervice. Is it impoffible then to deftroy this inhuman practice, which, notwithftanding the efforts of feveral princes, remains to this day? By no means—firft of all let the fencing fchools be fuppreffed; in thefe places, young fellows foon grow idle and corrupt, acquire a wrangling fpirit, and a bullying behaviour, which is a plague to fociety, and moft frequently proves fatal to themfelves. The Knights of the age of chivalry, whom we are apt to call barbarous and ignorant, were lefs fo in this refpect than ourfelves. They exercifed at arms, but only with a view to encourage an art which ftrengthed their bodies, and rendered them more active and redoubtable in fight. But of what advantage is the art of fencing among us? what good could an army of fencing mafters do in repelling an invafion? If, then, this art avails nothing to the defence of a country, and is dangerous to the citizens, why not fupprefs it, and prohibit the practice? Except fire arms, the cutlafs is the only weapon that the troops make ufe of in actual fervice, and why cannot the management of it be learnt in fchools, appropriated to the corps in fervice only, and the carrying of it be forbidden to all other citizens, and even (as is the practice of fome nations) to the military themfelves, when not upon real duty. Let no officer be expelled from his corps for having refufed a challenge, but rather let fuch a conduct be the means of his advancement, efpecially if his fkill and bravery have been tried on other occafions. The man who is capable of facrificing vulgar prejudices to the good of his country, certainly merits its thanks; and whoever fhould reproach fuch a one, ought to be driven away or punifhed, be he officer or foldier. Whoever fends a challenge, ought to fuffer difhonour and difgrace, and the commanders fhould be alfo obliged, under fevere penalties, not to fuffer duellifts in the army, any more than they now do men that refufe to fight. Such officers as have difputes with each other, fhould be compelled to fubmit them to the decifion of their equals: this would have far more effect upon a giddy young fellow, than being obliged to fight a duel, where

L

Legions of birds and quadrupedes will not here be allowed to destroy the husbandman's fields with impunity; and he, as well as the rich and great, may spread his nets for fish, in the rivers that wind thro' his meadows.

The indolent, passive character of these people, would ,it is true, lead one to suspect that they will never arrive to the power and importance that so many natural advantages seem to promise. But then it must be considered that this national character arises from custom, climate and a manner of living which will one day be greatly changed: a regular, retired manner of life, ignorant of the impulses of ambition, unacquainted with extravagant pleasure, and not exposed to great and sudden changes of fortune, unaccustomed to variety, and less laboriously than agreeably spent, cannot have that activity and energy which pressing necessities and unruly passions excite and keep up. Food, weak and unsubstantial ; drink without a mixture of spirit, rather dissolving than digestive; an air impregnated with humid particles, from the evaporation of the forests, must necessarily slacken and relax the nerves, give a slower, but more regular circulation to the blood, and consequently render the feelings less acute, the imagination less lively, and less animated, the humour more cold and dull, but not so inconstant as with us. Yet, when a more numerous population shall have levelled these immense forests, and laid open the soil to the genial influence of the sun, when the air shall have become more free and thin, and new plantations, and an extensive commerce shall have made the use of spirituous liquors more common, when the people shall settle nearer together and have more intercourse than at present ; then the passions will awake and be roused to action, and the Americans will show at once what they are to be.

But what a spectacle do these settlements even now already exhibit to our view, considering that they are but of little more than a century standing, and have been constantly under the controul of English policy, always suspicious and tyrannical, which seized the fruits of their industry, and rendered itself the sole possessor of their commerce !

Spacious and level roads already traverse the vastly extended forests of this country ; large and costly buildings have been raised, either for the meeting of the representatives of the States, for an asylum to the defenders of their country, in distress, or for the convenience of instructing young citizens in language, arts and science.
Thefe

be might flatter himself that his skill and dexterity would bring him off conqueror. The French, would not be reputed less brave, for not having private fights among themselves. The Gauls, the Greeks, and the Romans at no time cut each others throats for an offensive word, and yet we cry them up for prodigies of courage.——Such easy and simple methods would infallibly change our manners, and bring about a revolution in morals that would do more honour to the present age, than the most sublime discoveries.

Thefe laft, which are for the moft part endowed with confiderable poffeffions and revenues, are alfo furnifhed with libraries, and are under the direction of able mafters, invited hither from different parts of Europe: fhip yards are eftablifhed in all their ports, and they already rival the beft artifts of the old world in point of naval architecture; numerous mines have been opened, and they have now feveral founderies for cafting of cannon, which are in no refpect inferior to our own; and if the height of the architects fkill has not yet covered their waters with thofe prodigious bridges, which are wont to be extended over the waves, and unite the oppofite fhores of large rivers, as with us, ftill induftry and perfeverance has fupplied the want thereof; planks laid upon beams, lafhed together with ftout rings, and which may be taken apart at the pleafure of the builder are by their buoyancy as folid and ufeful as our firmeft works, defigned for the fame ends. In other places when a river is too deep for fixing the foundation of a bridge on its bottom, a ftout mafs of timber work is thrown over in a curve line, fupported only at the extremities, the internal ftrength of the ftructure upholding it in every other part. Tifonderoga, § the taking of which by the Englifh, covered the

Americans

§ *The Europeans have been greatly miftaken with regard to the motives and behaviour of the American leaders on this celebrated occafion. Their whole force confifted of very little more than 2500 men, while that of the enemy was at leaft 10,000. The poft could not have been evacuated with any honour till the force and numbers of the enemy were afcertained, and this, from a variety of caufes, was not done in this inftance till they were almoft upon the fpot. Thus an abandonment of the place became abfolutely neceffary, and in fuch circumftances the retreat that was made, under General St. Clair, was certainly in every fenfe proper and preferable to waiting the event of an affault, in which, from the inequality of numbers, the place would in all probability, have been carried, and not a foldier left to oppofe the progrefs of the enemy fouthward. The army at Charleftown, in 1780, were nearly in fimilar circumftances with that at Ticonderoga, in 1777; what blood and devaftation would have been faved, had the army, that afterwards were made prifoners in that place, been withdrawn from the garrifon for the defence of the country, inftead of waiting to be furrounded by the enemy. The world now at length, gives General St. Clair full credit for the generous and difinterefted part he acted at Ticonderoga. While he was yet in his intrenchments, he obferved to Colonel Varrick, one of his officers, with a magnanimity that cannot be fufficiently admired—" If I evacuate the place, my character will be ruined; if I remain here, the army will be loft; but for the fafety of the army I am determined to evacuate it, altho' it will give fuch an alarm as has not happened in the country fince the war commenced."* TRANSLATOR.

Americans with confusion, still proved to their astonished enemies, to what a pitch this industrious talent could be carried.

Every house and dwelling contains within itself almost all the original and most necessary arts: the hand that traces out the furrow, knows also how to give the shapeless block of wood what form it pleases, how to prepare the hides of cattle for use, and extract spirit from the juice of fruits. The young rural maiden,† whose charming complexion has not been turned tawny by the burning rays of the sun, or withered by blasting winds, upon whom pale misery has never stamped its hateful impressions, knows how to spin wool, cotton, flax, and afterwards weave them into cloth. Iron conductors are seen every where upon the buildings, which while they preserve the inhabitants from the fatal effects of lightning, immortalize the memory of Franklin, that venerable sage, who is the admiration of the Parisians; and shew at the same time how much they are disposed to profit by his inventions.

When the illegal, oppressive acts were framed, and sent over to destroy their privileges, with what prudence, resolution and courage did they not unite to defend-them!—and here we ought to pause, and fix our attention, to form a proper judgment of the Americans. Men, scattered through extensive countries, different in climate, and clashing in their interests and modes of worship, to the wonder of the whole world, formed associations, which coincided as exactly in their decisions, as if the whole matter had been preconcerted. Great-Britain vainly flattered herself, that by shutting up the port of Boston, she had effectually intimidated these provinces, and raised ruinous dissentions among them; yet, after this arbitrary act, their complaints were but the more urgent, and the common danger did but strengthen their union the more: the maritime towns in the neighbourhood of Boston, instead of being dazzled with the immense advantages which were promised them, viewed the measure with indignation and horror. The town of Salem, to which the privileges of the Bostonians were now transferred, wrote thus to the Governor of the province:

"We are deeply affected at the public calamities; and the "miseries of our brethren, in the capital of the province give us "the greatest concern; we will continue to hope however that your "excellency will do your endeavour to lighten the accumulated "mischiefs that have fallen upon that unhappy people. Some "may imagine that the shutting up the harbour of Boston will turn "the whole commerce of that place into our channel, and be "greatly to our profit; but Nature, when she formed our port, "refused it equal advantages, and has not afforded us those con- "veniencies that would enable us to become rivals. Besides, we "have

† *It is evident that the author in this place, as well as in many others, is drawing a parallel between the condition of the American peasantry, and those of France, and several other countries of Europe.* TRANSLATOR.

" have not renounced every idea of juſtice and all the ſentiments of
" humanity, in entertaining the baſe thought of growing rich
" and making fortunes out of the ruins of our neighbours : &c.

Virginia reſolved, " That an attack made upon one colony, to
oblige it to ſubmit to arbitrary taxation, was equally injurious to
all the reſt, and threatened them with the total loſs of their privileges." The deciſions of Rhode-Iſland, where the weight of arbitrary power was moſt felt, were not leſs bold ; but thoſe of Maryland, a province in the hands of powerful proprietors, ſurpaſſed
them ſtill. All the reſt of the continent manifeſted the ſame firm-
neſs, and eſtabliſhed every where committees of correſpondence
with the general Congreſs.

And thus this prohibitory bill, that was publiſhed and laviſhly
diſſeminated through the country, far from ſpreading a univerſal
conſternation, had only, ſays the Engliſh hiſtorian, the effect
which the poets attribute to the torches of the Furies, that of burning and conſuming in every place where they happened to paſs.

New acts, relative to the lodging of the troops in the province
of Maſſachuſetts-Bay, completed the general indignation : they
now thought of nothing but ſhutting up the ports, making contri-
butions to ſuccour their ſuffering brethren in Boſton, and holding
a general Congreſs. In Boſton, the committee of correſpondence
paſſed an act, in which they obliged themſelves, in the moſt ſolemn
manner, by taking God to witneſs, to abſtain from all commercial intercourſe with Great-Britain, until the repeal of the prohibitory port act, and whatever elſe militated againſt their privileges ;
not to conſume or purchaſe any articles imported ſince the laſt of
Auguſt,—not to trade with thoſe who did import,—to renounce all
connexion with ſuch as ſhould refuſe to ſubſcribe to this agreement,
and publiſh their names, to be held in everlaſting diſgrace.

The ſeveral provinces ſtrove who ſhould be foremoſt in entering
into this league. In vain did General Gage, Governor of Maſſachuſetts-Bay, declare it, by his proclamation, illegal, deſtructive,
contrary to the fealty they owed the king, tending to deſtroy the le-
gal authority of the parliament of England, and injurious to the
public peace and ſecurity ; in vain did he employ threats, and order the judges to ſeize upon thoſe who ſhould ſubſcribe it, countenance it, or have any ſhare in publiſhing it.

Virginia, in addition to her more early determinations, now reſolved, that ſhe would import no more ſlaves from Africa, or the
Weſt-Indies ; and no Britiſh manufactures, after the firſt of November, if their grievances were not redreſſed by the 15th of Auguſt,
1775 ; that after this period, ſhe would not export tobacco or any
other merchandize to Great Britain, and that to ſupply her own
neceſſities, ſhe would cultivate thoſe productions moſt neceſſary,
and raiſe and multiply herds of cattle. Maryland, and the two
Carolinas, took the ſame meaſures ; and at Newport, this ſentence
was every where ſtuck up——*Unite or die.*

the

The people of the town of Marblehead, whose harbour was best
situated to profit by the shutting up of Boston, generously offered
to the Bostonians their town, their port, and supplies of provisions;
proposed to be present at the loading and unloading of their effects,
and to transact all their business for them, without expecting a
farthing of reward.

Their charters gave the Americans a right to choose their own
representatives. But General Gage, in violation thereof, received
from the court of London, a list of thirty-nine persons appointed to
sit in council; thirty-four of whom took their seats. But the people immediately declared them enemies to their country, threatened to treat them as such, and pronounced them incapable of
holding their places.

The lawyers and juries of the province, at the opening of the
courts, refused to take the usual oath, or to have any connexion
with them, while the registers of the courts asked pardon of their
country, in the public papers, for having issued warrants for sum-
moning the jurors to attend, with promises not to commit the same
fault again; declaring, at the same time, that they would never
forgive themselves for it, altho' their countrymen should: Entrance
into the courts of justice was refused the judges; they were surrounded by the populace, wherever they went, were pursued into
their very houses, and forced at last to conceal themselves, not only
from the public, but from each other.

The old constitution being thus annulled by act of parliament,
the people at the same time rejecting the new one, there was no
longer law nor government in the province of Massachusetts-Bay:
However, even in this state of anarchy, they committed no acts of
excess to be reproached with; such an influence had the old laws
upon their minds, at the moment they were to be annihilated!

At length, the general Congress opened at Philadelphia, on the
fifth of September, 1774, and published in the most open and
solemn manner, the sentiments, the views and the resources of the
confederated provinces. The instructions given them by their con-
stituents, bore a striking likeness to their character, and the different modes of thinking among them; but were perfectly consonant
in the most material points, and tended to the same purpose.

In their address to General Gage they complain of the oppressive acts of parliament, of his rigorous mode of executing
them, of the fortifications raised at Boston, the plundered property of individuals, the disorderly conduct of his troops, and
the cutting off the intercourse between the town and country.

They published at the same time, a declaration of the immutable
natural rights of the provinces, the principles of the English
constitution, and their different charters. " No one, say they,
can dispose of our lives, our liberties and our property without our
consent; the colonies have yielded up these unalienable rights to
no power whatever; our ancestors, from the time of their emi-
gration, have enjoyed the privileges of English born subjects; by
their

their emigrating to America they, by no means, gave up or loft thefe rights ; and, confidered as fuch fubjects, they cannot but have a fhare in the legiflative council, and fince they are not admitted to, and cannot be reprefented in, the parliament of England, their legiflative power muft exift in their provincial affemblies ; they cannot therefore be taxed arbitrarily, or without their own confent, and if they enjoy equal privileges with the mother country, they have alfo the fame right to be tried by their peers : befides, all thefe privileges have been confirmed by royal charters, and recognized by acts of parliament."——They then declare, unanimoufly that " if thefe grievances are not redreffed, they will import no more commodities from Great Britain ;" and afterward enter into fome difcuffions relative to the conduct of the merchants, the encouragement of manufactures, and the confumption of commodities.

They likewife addreffed a petition to his majefty, a memorial to the people of Great Britain, an addrefs to the colonies in general, and another to Canada.

In the petition to his majefty, they obferve, that an army is kept up in the colonies in time of peace, without their confent, that a naval force was employed to countenance unjuft impofitions upon trade ; that the authority of commander in chief, and Brigadier General, was become abfolute in every government in America ; that the commanding *General* was in time of peace, nominated *Governor* of a colony ; and that the number of expenfive, oppreffive officers was unneceffarily and prodigioufly increafed ; that the judges were become wholly dependant upon the crown for their falaries, and the duration of their commiffions, that the agents of the people were difcountenanced, and inftructions given to prevent the payment of their falaries, &c. In fhort they omitted nothing that could difplay their attachment and fubmiffion to their fovereign, or their love and veneration for their mother country.—They next tell him, " We have inherited from our anceftors that paffionate love of liberty, which placed your illuftrious family on the throne." They then go on to befeech him by all that is moft facred, by the interefts of his kingdom, by his own, by the fecurity and profperity of the laws, by the happinefs of his fubjects, whofe father he is, not to fuffer fuch intimate bonds of affection to be broken afunder in expectation of certain events, which, altho' they might poffibly turn out at laft to his wifh, would never compenfate for the inevitable loffes that would attend them.

In the memorial addreffed to the people of Britain, they bring into view the rights they ought to enjoy as free men, citizens and colonifts, the fmall regard they entertain for the prefent Englifh miniftry, the attachment they had always fhown for their mother country, the numerous fervices they had rendered her the laft war, and the taxes with which they were burdened upon her account, and which were foolifhly fquandered upon court favourites. They prove undeniably that fuccefs againft them would be as

dangerous

dangerous to the liberties of Great-Britain as to thofe of America.
" America once fubjected, fay they, would herfelf become the
" inftrument of fubjecting you."

They laftly build their hopes of a re-eftablifhment of peace and
harmony, friendfhip and brotherly affection among all his majefty's fubjects, upon the greatnefs and juftice of the Britifh nation,
by choofing a wife, independent parliament, animated with a
love of the public good, and a defire to defend their violated
rights againft a wicked and ill defigning miniftry.

In their addrefs to the Canadians, they difcover the greateft
caution and difcretion, and make ufe of fuch arguments as are
moft conformable to the genius and interefts of that people. They
demonftrate from reafon, from facts, from the teftimony of the
moft celebrated writers, that in becoming Englifh fubjects, they
participate in all their prerogatives; they prove that the Quebec
act, deprived them of all thefe; that they had no longer a political
exiftence; that their property, and even their perfons were become
fubjected to the will and the caprice of a tyrannical minifter.

They fhew them that, forming a fmall people in comparifon of
their numerous and powerful neighbours, it is their intereft and
happinefs to have the united colonies for their fteady friends, fince
nature had joined their refpective countries together by an indiffolu-
ble connexion, and feparated them alike from their tyrannical
oppreffors by extenfive tracts of ocean. " Difference of religion,
" obferve they, cannot be an obftacle to our union ; fuch differ-
" ence exifts in the *Swifs Cantons*, and yet they are not the lefs
" united."——They go on to affure them, that it is the wifh of
the colonies to confider them as allies ; and that fuch an alliance
has been unanimoufly affented to in their affemblies ; that a violation of *their* rights fhall be looked upon as an infult offered to
their own, and that they now invited them to accede to a confe-
deracy, the object of which was the fecurity of the natural and
civil privileges of the members of the community.

This invitation of the general Congrefs, and the addreffes,
containing quite a new political fyftem, were revered almoft as
much as the Bible among the people, who adhered ftrictly to the
opinions therein contained, in every particular : they flattered
themfelves that fuch petitions and addreffes as thefe could not fail of
bringing about fome favourable changes in England; but when
they found that they had no other effect, and were anfwered no other
way, than by an act prohibiting the exportation of warlike ftores
from Great Britain to New-England, then it was that pacific
meafures were totally given up ;——bodies of militia were immediately formed, regulations for difcipline were made, and means
taken to provide arms and ammunition. They encouraged the
erecting of powder-mills, manufactures of falt-petre and fmall arms
were alfo fet on foot. Some of the provinces went fo far, as to
feize upon the ammunition and arms in the public ftores; and
thus it turned out that the acts of parliament, the feverity of which
was

was meant to reduce the colonies to tranquillity, only ferved to increafe the flames of animofity and difcord.

All hopes of reconciliation being now at an end, feveral trifling acts of hoftility foreboded more confiderable ones to be near at hand.

England muft have feen with aftonifhment, the colonies difcuffing their rights with fo much boldnefs and truth, taking meafures fo wifely, and difcovering fuch undaunted refolution: but what muft have been her fears, when after her formidable armaments had arrived to fubdue them, fhe faw them dare to advance, and difpute every inch of ground with thefe numerous veteran forces?

Men who had never learnt to obey, always accuftomed to the peace and quiet of a rural life, bred up in abundance, of a flow and peaceable difpofition, whofe breafts the very idea of human blood chilled with horror; could fhe have conceived that fuch as thefe were capable of abandoning their wonted dwellings, fubmitting to fevere fubordination, defpifing hunger, the inclemency of the weather, fupporting long and painful marches, giving and receiving death with intrepidity, and all againft a nation fo terrible to them by her ancient fame and late fuccefles? Could fhe have believed that they would attempt any thing againft her, when, deftitute of experienced commanders, and unprovided with arms or ammunition, they found themfelves obliged to oppofe a warlike enemy, long practiced in battles, and abundantly fupplyed with every thing that could enfure fuccefs?——England, no doubt, actuated by an ambitious policy, was thoroughly perfuaded at firft that a fmall number of her troops would fuffice to fight and fubdue the Americans: and if thefe troops, with the immenfe hofts that fucceeded them, failed in their endeavours and were conquered, I will be bold to fay it is a phenomenon in the political world that no empire or kingdom has feen the like of in paft ages, and perhaps nothing like it will ever happen again. *

We in France, were not at all furprized to fee the new raifed American legions fo often flying before the enemy, difperfing themfelves in the woods, or vanifhing at the approach of the foe; but we were thunderftruck when we beheld them re-uniting, fhowing themfelves once more in force, and always fupporting hunger, wounds,

M

* *Hiftory, it is true, furnifhes us with feveral examples of provinces fhaking off the yoke of a great empire, and of a comparatively inconfiderable number of men gaining victories over large armies; but fuch revolutions were brought about, and fuch victories gained by warlike nations, in thofe times when valour ftood in the place of numbers and fkill. We have never, till now, read of men, harraffed with internal factions, unprovided with the means, and ignorant of the fcience of war, gaining the day over a brave and enlightened nation, as fertile in refources, and of as enterprizing a genius as any in the world.*

wounds, and other evils incident to war, with patience and
courage. The more the haughty English had studied and observed
the genius, the inclinations and the resources of their colonists,
the more they had to encourage themselves to rely upon the
success of their arms. Yet never were the plans of a nation more
completely frustrated. With regard to America, their wisest men
reasoned like children: the object was too great for their compre-
hension, and as they had hitherto only viewed the Americans in
the calms of rural and commercial life, they forgot, or did not
know, or would not recollect, that native *cowardice* itself, for with
that they falsely upbraided them, can be roused into heroism at the
prospect of approaching ruin—and thus their folly and ambition
has transferred a glorious sovereignty to the western world, which
will we hope contribute largely in its effects to the happiness and
well being of mankind in general, but philosophy lets us see,
that it will take several ages to complete the great revolution which
has been begun in our day.

You have hitherto seen the Americans acting rather from an
impulse of cool reason than sentiment, better pleased with reflecting than thinking, and taken up with useful rather than agreeable things; and for this reason, legislation, politics, natural
and mechanical philosophy may make considerable progress,
among them, while the fine arts remain unknown, and while
even poetry, which in all other nations has preceded the sciences,
forbears to raise her lofty and animated strains.

Their towns, their villages, their places of abode may afford
ease, health and regularity, but will present nothing that interests
and refreshes the imagination ; here are no trees planted through
the country in straight lines, or bent into bowers to refresh the
traveller with their shade: here are no gardens contrived with
ingenious arrangements, where a pleasant symmetry and a happy
mixture of flowers inebriate the senses, and enchant the soul;
neither have they any theatrical shows or dances, or those public
exhibitions which might give us an idea of their felicity and cheer-
ful disposition— and yet how is it that patriotism could unite such
men, and make them capable of such surprising efforts? It was
undoubtedly owing, among other things, to the impost upon tea,
which by depriving them in an instant of that article, severely
distressed every individual ; it may also be attributed in part to
the intolerant spirit of Presbyterianism, which has for so long a
time been sowing the seeds of discord between them and the
mother country ; and to the too limited state of their commerce,
which with the productions of one of the richest soils in the world,
has scarcely yet supplied them with what we would call the most
common necessaries of life ; likewise to their newspapers, which cir-
culating through all parts, spread alarms every where, and presented the most dismal prospects to their view: but this critical moment, as I have already remarked, was not attended with acts of
violence and cruelty ; it was, on the contrary, comparatively, a
                                                            season

feafon of calmnefs and reflexion.————This revolution, the immediate period of which is advancing with hafty ftrides, deprives our enemies of at leaft three millions of fubjects, and a commerce that was daily adding to their ftrength and importance; but ours will become more open, liberal, and extenfive than ever, and we may even build fhips in America at a much cheaper rate than we have hitherto purchafed them in the north of Europe, where they are alfo more difficult to be procured. We fhall get our tobacco at an eafy barter, and not throw annually an immenfe balance of ready money into the hands of a rival nation, to purchafe it; and our iflands will always have a demand for the American lumber to contain their rum, molaffes and other productions.

It has often been faid, that we of France ought to be upon our guard, leaft at the firft appearance of peace the national prejudices of the Americans fhould incline them to renew their old connexions with the mother country, forget our fervices, and break the alliance.—But we have little reafon to apprehend this, when we confider that the Englifh have been too long fhedding blood in thefe countries, and too long plundering the inhabitants, for them to think of regaining their real friendfhip very eafily. The Englifhman, who will long confider the American in the light of a flave efcaped from the fangs of his nation, will confequently for fome time affect an air of fuperiority, even after a peace; and contempt, which is more difficult to be got over by a generous fpirit than open hatred, will not eafily be forgiven by the much injured American.

The Congrefs, whofe refolves have always been dictated by wifdom and equity, and whofe decifions have never been blamed by any, will not, furely, tarnifh their honour and glory by a want of fidelity to their firft ally; they will not erect a monument to infamy, upon which the whole world, and all future ages would read————*France firft acknowledged the Independence of America, and made the firft treaty of alliance with her, fupplied her with ammunition, affifted her with her treafures, and defended her with her fleets and armies: America ungratefully violated her oaths, and burft afunder the ties of friendfhip, as foon as fhe could do it without danger to herfelf.*

Altho' fhe fhould be capable, during the prefent war, of abftracting her quarrel from ours, and making a peace before us, ftill what would be the refult? her power would no longer be incorporated with that of Great Britain, and fo our great object would be neverthelefs accomplifhed. Peace in America would likewife fave us the keeping on foot an expenfive army in this country, the loan of immenfe fums, and fupplying them with large quantities of warlike ftores for their own troop.

If we muft extend our views into futurity, it is more rational to apprehend that the vaft confumption of rum, fugar and coffee among the Americans, will incline them at one time or another to

make

make attempts upon our islands that they may have such articles at a cheaper rate ; but can the produce of these, how immense soever you may suppose it, be once put in competition with the lives of those men, which these destructive climates deprive us of every year, and would deprive them of in like manner ; or with that corruption of morals which is constantly ebbing back from thence into Europe ?

The prosperity of states and empires depends only upon manners and population, and to these every thing else must be sacrificed— O Americans, what calamities will attend you if the allurements of such a conquest shall one day seduce you to unite with Britain, and arm against us : the vice and wickedness which would flow from thence into the bosom of your country, and which would most fatally suspend the progress of your population, would also avenge us amply for your bold attempts.——But I will not, I cannot indulge the idea.—Occupied wholly in the rural employments of multiplying your flocks, extending he bounds of your farms, and improving the wild face of your native region, you will not go armed with fire and sword to ravage and conquer regions that rise in the midst of the seas, beneath the sickly fervours of a torrid sky.—Those happy plains which you inhabit, and which surround you on every side, extend even beyond your fondest wishes, and ask not a waste of blood, but the hand of industry, to open and disclose their inexhaustible treasures. The nature of the climate may perhaps refuse those productions which European luxury has taught you to esteem the real necessaries of life, but your woods, your grains, your fisheries, and your numerous flocks will always be sufficient to procure you these.

Their manners and climate will not only for a long time incline the Americans to peace, but their political situation will probably still increase this rational propensity ; they are not surrounded by restless, ambitious nations, who will oblige them to be incessantly armed to guard against their designs; altho' consisting of distinct bodies, they will never be exposed to those frequent altercations among themselves which vex the republics of Europe ; their respective rights are too clearly established, too generally received, and too intimately connected not to tend constantly to the destruction of the oppressor.

Necessity, fear, and ignorance have given birth to many warlike nations, and Europe would never have been engaged so constantly in wars, had she not been originally peopled by barbarians, fugitives, foreigners, and such as possessed different manners, and were violently opposed to each other, both by prejudice and interest ; and if she is still in this unhappy situation, it is only the consequence of those miserable ages of darkness and ignorance. The immense variety of different forms of worship will probably operate as the first cause of future dissentions in America ; altho' it is to this very circumstance they owe their rapid increase of power, and which will still contribute to their aggrandisement : but to

suppose

fuppofe that toleration can be prejudicial to the profperity of ftates, is, whatever you may think of it, very far from the received opinion of our time.

As long as men live at a diftance from each other, toleration cannot be attended with any ill confequences, becaufe in fuch a detached ftate, they are lefs liable to clafh in their opinions, and confequently lefs fubject to divifions. But when a country becomes better peopled, when families fettle nearer together, and the communication among them is enlarged, the clafh of opinions becomes more frequent, violent and dangerous ; and then is the time for religious factions to fpring up. Two flourifhing ftates, England and Holland, fubfift, neverthelefs, to this day, although they tolerate a multitude of fects. The firft, wholly taken up in commercial fpeculations, permits all its members to remain in ignorance and indifference, except in what relates to gain. On the other hand, the neceffity of an intercourfe with all nations, renders the Hollander inattentive to the difputes of his fectaries, efpecially when he confiders, that the power of his country, at beft precarious, would foon crumble to pieces without their fupport. The fame caufes operate upon the Englifh nation, but not fo powerfully, becaufe they are not fo generally commercial ; and becaufe the people, being of a lefs laborious turn, and lefs generally fpeculative than the Dutch, poffefs in a greater degree the powers of reafoning and reflecting, and are more taken up with their doctrinal opinions : fo that all the fects in England are fo many rivals and enemies to each other, and their churches perpetually refound with the moft illiberal and outrageous differtations and difcourfes. This hatred of each other, would often be attended with fatal effects, were it not for the venerable majefty of the Catholic faith, which is a perpetual terror to their imaginations, and againft which, as a common enemy, they all unite, as well as againft the menacing power of France, which has almoft always kept them and their nation fufficiently employed.

But America, who will be always more at peace abroad, and will never be indebted for her greatnefs and power to external and momentary caufes, and who will one day include, in her various fertile countries, vaft numbers of rich, independent, reafoning, cavilling citizens, will have more to fear from the difference of religious opinions. Even now, or very lately, the writings and fermons of their minifters, were as much calculated to attack and ridicule their rivals, as to edify their hearers ; and Philadelphia, the center of tolerancy, has feen its fectaries fupporting their religious privileges by blows and violence, Different times and circumftances may render fuch feuds of the utmoft ill confequence.

The more the various religions of mankind are enlightened, of a more intolerant fpirit they commonly are. *Paganifm*, without any coherency or fixed principles, admitted and tolerated every mode of worfhip ; *Judaifm*, more rational and better connected, rejected all ; *Mahometifm* would never have been known in the
world

world, or grown to what it is, had not its *author* expressly forbid toleration ; and the *christian world* has always discountenanced it, except only such sects as were unsettled, and wavering in their doctrinal opinions. Philosophy, whose business it is to unite men, and moderate their passions, has certainly inclined them in time past to civil toleration, but aspiring to examine into, and judge of every thing, it at first necessarily occasioned speculative, and afterwards political, intolerancy ; because the laws cannot be long indifferent in those matters, in which the passions of men are particularly interested.

The happiest government, and which promises the most lasting prosperity, is that which connects all the members of a society in the same faith, and the same form of worship. True policy ought, then, constantly to endeavour to recall mankind to a unity of faith ; but a desire of attracting foreigners, and the speedy peopling of a country, has tempted several states to transgress this principle, by opening an asylum to all religions without exception. Now, if it can be demonstrated, that a well circumstanced nation, where they all profess one faith, doubles its number of inhabitants every twenty years, would it not be more honourable to live in religious harmony, with such a degree of population, than to be forever quarrelling about creeds and tenets, and torn by religious divisions ? This would be serving the present age and posterity both at once.

People, whom edicts of toleration invite into a country, thereby undoubtedly acquire those rights and privileges, which the legislative authority cannot infringe without injustice. Louis the fourteenth, by revoking the edict of Nantes, destroyed at once in his kingdom, the principle of intestine divisions, and this perhaps (as some have said) might have been good policy, but not the most just ; because contracts made with Heretics, are not at all the less sacred for that.

The ruler of a country ought to consider himself as the father of his subjects also ; out of a principle of tenderness, he should constantly aim to strengthen the bands which connect his numerous family ; and can there be a more powerful one than a religion which inspires the same sentiments, prescribes the same duties, and promises the same rewards ?—How many millions live and die enemies to each other, merely on account of diversity of opinion in religious matters ! but the man who feels the influence of true virtue and catholicism, who keeps eternity constantly in view, and pants for a more intimate union with the pure spirit of the Divinity, perceives his affections expanding, and his heart glowing with rapture, when he can entertain rational hopes of enjoying the future friendship of his fellow men on the other side of the grave, in the regions beyond this transitory state of being.

One of the most affecting scenes, and which will do the most honour to the world, will be when all nations shall unite in erecting the same temples for the service of the Deity, and tuning the

the

fame anthems to his praife; and philofophy, which pretends to render mankind happier and better, ought to direct all her views and efforts to this great end : But can fhe flatter herfelf with paving the way to fuch a revolution in fentiment, while fhe employs herfelf folely to overturn and deftroy all religions whatever ?— Before fhe enterprized fo boldly, fhe fhould have offered the world a fyftem of faith built upon better foundations, comprizing a greater number of moral truths; and which would have pointed out more diftinctly the extent and limits of human reafon, than that already received; that fhould have more inclined the human race to the love of virtue and the dread of vice ; which would have been better fuited to all times and all places, to all conditions, and all temper.

By acting in a different manner, fhe refembles a law giver, who difliking the laws of the nation over which he prefides, fhould abolifh them without offering another, and a better fyftem of legiflation in their ftead ; or a phyfician, who fhould forbid his patients the ufe of food, which perhaps might not be altogether falutary, without once intimating what fhould be fubftituted of a lefs noxious quality.

Philofophy fhould confine her endeavours to the ftudy and examination of the pretences that every religion makes to be thought the true one, to mark what they have moft perfect or moft defective in their ufages and forms, their difcipline and their doctrines : to keep aloof from thofe rafh difputes and controverfies, which render men neither better nor wifer, and to fhew the world, that mild perfuafion and good example, will reclaim mankind much fooner to the fide of truth and virtue, than an imperious, infolent mode of conviction, which can only irritate.

Perhaps this deftructive and ambitious philofophy of our day will be fucceeded fome time or another by one of a more moderate and conciliating temper. At this moment new empires are burfting into exiftence, and mankind will unavoidably begin to perceive the neceffity of exercifing their *reafon* to a better purpofe than heretofore; more connected by commerce, they will receive and communicate knowledge with greater facility than ever; the genius and talents of one individual man, and the fpirit of party divifions will no longer have the fame influence as formerly ; the fhameful errors of fanatics, and the contracted notions of bigots and devotees will now vanifh, and though they fhould revive under a thoufand different forms, this new and rational philofophy will, notwithftanding, at laft recall all the nations of the world to a unity of fentiment and worfhip: perhaps the hope of fuch an event may be vain, but the idea is certainly flattering and comfortable to the human mind. I am, &c.

THE END.

APPENDIX.

CONTAINING

I. *Copy of a Letter from General Washington to Count de Grasse.*

Williamsburg, September 26, 1781.

SIR,

I AM unable to describe to your Excellency, the painful anxi-ety under which I have laboured, since the reception of the letter you did me the honour to write me of the 23d instant. The motions of the naval force under your command, which your Ex-cellency says may possibly happen, since the information commu-nicated to you by the Baron de Clozen, obliged me to point out the consequences that may follow; and warmly to urge a perfe-verance in the plan agreed upon between us. Permit me, in the first place, to repeat to your Excellency, that the attempt upon York, under the protection of your shipping, is as certain of suc-cess as a superior force and a superiority of measures can render any military operation; that the duration of the siege may be exactly ascertained; and that the capture of the British army is a matter so important in itself, and in its consequences, that it must greatly tend to bring an end to the war, and put our allied arms in cer-tain possession of the most inestimable advantages.

If

If your Excellency quits the Bay, an accefs is open to relieve York, of which the enemy will inftantly avail themfelves. The confequences of this will be not only the difgrace of abandoning a defign on which are founded the faireft hopes of the allied forces, after a prodigious expence, fatigue and exertions; but the probable difbanding of the whole army ; for the prefent feat of war being fuch, as abfolutely precludes the ufe of waggons, from the great number of large rivers which interfect the country, there will be a total want of provifions, unlefs this inconvenience is remedied by water carriage. This province has been fo exhaufted by the ravages of the enemy, and by the fupport already given to our forces, that fubfiftence muft be drawn from a diftance, and that can be done only by a fleet fuperior in the Bay.

I earneftly beg your Excellency would confider, that if, by moving your fleet from the fituation agreed on, we lofe the prefent opportunity, we fhall never hereafter have it in our power to ftrike fo decifive a ftroke, that the Britifh will labour without intermiffion to fortify a place fo ufeful to their fhipping ; and that then the period of an honourable peace will be farther diftant than ever.

The confidence I have in your Excellency's manly fpirit and naval talents leaves me no doubt that the confideration of the confequences that muft follow your departure from the Bay will determine you to ufe all poffible means for the good of the common caufe. From the affurances of the moft expert failors, I am perfuaded that your Excellency may take fuch a pofition in the Bay, as to leave nothing to be apprehended from an attempt of the Englifh fleet; that this pofition will at the fame time facilitate the operations of the fiege, fecure the tranfportation of our provifions by water, and accelerate our approaches by landing our heavy artillery and warlike neceffaries in York River almoft clofe to o- trenches.

The force faid to have arrived under Admiral Digby, as t. news comes from the Britifh themfelves, may not only be exagge rated, but perhaps abfolutely falfe; but fuppofing it to be tru. their whole force united cannot be fuch as to give them any hope of fuccefs in the attacking your fleet. If the pofition for you. fhips to lie at an anchor, which we agreed upon, has fince appeared impracticable, there is ftill another meafure may be adopted ; which, though much inferior as to the fecurity and facility it will give to our land operations, may ftill be of advantage to our affairs. The meafure, I mean, is to cruife off the Bay, fo as to keep the Capes always in fight, and to prevent any Englifh veffels getting in.

Whatever plan you may adopt, I am to prefs your Excellency to perfevere in the fcheme fo happily concerted between us ; but if you fhould find infurmountable obftacles in the way, let me ultimately beg of you not to relinquifh the laft mentioned alternative of preventing all veffels from the enemy entering the Bay of Chefapeak.

N   The

" The British Admiral may manœuvre his fleet, and endeavour to draw you from the main object we have in view; but I can never believe, that he will seriously wish to bring on a general action with a fleet, whofe force, I will answer it, is superior to the moft exaggerated accounts we have of theirs. Passed experience has taught them not to hazard themselves with equal numbers ; and has drawn from them, though unwillingly, the moft respectful opinions of their enemy.

Permit me to add, that the absence of your fleet from the Bay, may fruftrate our defign upon the garrison at York. For in the prefent fituation of matters, Lord Cornwallis might evacuate the place with the lofs of his artillery, baggage, and a few men, facrifices ; which would be highly juftifiable from the defire of faving the body of the army.

The Marquis de la Fayette, who does me the honor to carry this letter to your Excellency, will explain to you better than any other perfon, or than I can do by letter, many particulars of our prefent pofition. Your Excellency is acquainted with his candour and talents, which entitles him to your confidence. I have ordered him not to pafs the Cape for fear of accident, in cafe you fhould be at fea. If this be fo, he will inclofe this difpatch in a letter from himfelf.

I have the honour to be, &c.

G. WASHINGTON.

II. *Copy of a Letter from Lieutenant-General Earl Cornwallis, to Sir Henry Clinton.*

York-Town, in Virginia, October 20, 1781.

SIR,

HAVE the mortification to inform your Excellency, that I have been forced to give up the pofts of York and Gloucefter, d to furrender the troops under my command, by Capitulation, the 19th inftant, as prifoners of war to the combined forces of America and France.

I never faw this poft in a very favourable light; but when I found I was to be attacked in it in fo unprepared a ftate, by fo powerful an army and artillery, nothing but the hopes of relief would have induced me to attempt its defence; for I would either have endeavoured to efcape to New-York, by rapid marches from the Gloucefter fide, immediately on the arrival of General Wafhington's troops at Williamfburg, or I would, notwithftanding the difparity of numbers, have attacked them in the open field, where it might have been juft poffible that fortune would have favoured the gallantry of the handful of troops under my command : but being affured by your Excellency's letter, that every poffible means would be tried by the navy and army to relieve us, I could not

think

think myfelf at liberty to venture on either of thofe defperate attempts: therefore after remaining two days in a ftrong pofition in front of this place, in hopes of being attacked, upon obferving that the enemy were taking meafures which could not fail of turning my left flank in a fhort time; and receiving, on the fecond evening, your letter of the 24th of September, informing me, that the relief would fail about the 5th of October, I withdrew within the works on the night of the 29th of September, hoping, by the labour and firmnefs of the foldiers, to protract the defence until you could arrive.

Every thing was to be expected from the fpirit of the troops, but every difadvantage attended their labour, as the works were to be continued under the enemy's fire, and our ftock of intrenching tools, which did not much exceed 400 when we began to work in the latter end of Auguft, was now much diminifhed.

The enemy broke ground on the night of the 30th and conftructed, on that night and the two following days and nights, two redoubts, which, with fome works that had belonged to our outward pofition, occupied a gorge between two creeks or ravines, which come from the river on each fide of the town. On the night of the 6th of October, they made their firft parallel, extending from its right on the river to a deep ravine on the left, nearly oppofite to the centre of this place, and embracing our whole left, at the diftance of fix hundred yards. Having perfected this parallel, their batteries opened on the evening of the 9th againft our left; and other batteries fired at the fame time againft a redoubt advanced over the creek upon our right and defended by about 120 men of the 23d regiment and marines, who maintained that poft with uncommon gallantry. The fire continued inceffant from heavy cannon, and from mortars and howitzers throwing fhells from fix to fixteen inches, until all our guns on the left were filenced, our works much damaged, and our lofs of men confiderable. On the night of the 11th they began their fecond parallel, about three hundred yards nearer to us. The troops being much weakened by ficknefs, as well as by the fire of the befiegers, and obferving that the enemy had not only fecured their flank, but proceeded in every refpect with the utmoft regularity and caution, I could not venture fo large forties as to hope from them any confiderable effect; but otherwife I did every thing in my power to interrupt this work, by opening new embrazures for guns, and keeping up a conftant fire with all the howitzers and fmall mortars that we could man. On the evening of the 14th they affaulted and carryed two redoubts that had been advanced about three hundred yards, for the purpofe of delaying their approaches, and covering our left flank, and during the night included them in their fecond parallel, on which they continued to work with the utmoft exertion. Being perfectly fenfible that our works could not ftand many hours after the opening of the batteries of that parallel, we not only continued a conftant fire with all our mortars, and every gun that could be

brought

brought to bear upon it; but, a little before day-break, on the morning of the 16th, I ordered a ſortie of about three hundred and fifty men, under the direction of Lieutenant-Colonel Abercromby, to attack two batteries which appeared to be in the greateſt forwardneſs, and to ſpike the guns. A detachment of guards, with the 80th company of grenadiers, under the command of Lieutenant-Colonel Lake attacked the one; and one of light infantry, under the command of Major Armſtrong, attacked the other; and both ſucceeded, by forcing the redoubts that covered them, ſpiking eleven guns, and killing or wounding about one hundred of the French troops who had the guard of that part of the trenches, and with little loſs on our ſide. This action, though extremely honourable to the officers and ſoldiers who executed it, proved of little public advantage; for the cannon having been ſpiked in a hurry, were ſoon rendered fit for ſervice again, and before dark the whole parallel and batteries appeared to be nearly complete. At this time we knew that there was no part of the whole front attacked, in which we could ſhew a ſingle gun, and our ſhells were nearly expended. I had therefore only to chooſe between preparing to ſurrender next day, or endeavouring to get off with the greateſt part of the troops; and I determined to attempt the latter, reflecting, that though it ſhould prove unſucceſsful in its immediate object, it might at leaſt delay the enemy in the proſecution of further enterpriſes. Sixteen large boats were prepared, and upon other pretexts were ordered to be in readineſs to receive troops preciſely at ten o'clock; with theſe I hoped to paſs the infantry during the night, abandoning our baggage and leaving a detachment to capitulate for the town's people and for the ſick and wounded; on which ſubject a letter was ready to be delivered to General Waſhington. After making my arrangements with the utmoſt ſecreſy, the light infantry, the greateſt part of the guards, and part of the 23d regiment, embarked at the hour appointed, and moſt of them landed at Glouceſter; but at this critical moment, the weather, from being moderate and calm, changed to a moſt violent ſtorm of wind and rain, and drove all the boats ſome of which had troops on board, down the river. It was ſoon evident that the intended paſſage was impracticable, and that the abſence of the boats rendered it equally impoſſible to bring back the troops which had paſſed, which I had ordered about two o'clock in the morning. In this ſituation, with my little force divided, the enemy's batteries opened at day-break. The paſſage between this place and Glouceſter was much expoſed; but the boats having now returned, they were ordered to bring back the troops which had paſſed during the night, and they joined us in the forenoon, without much loſs. Our works in the mean time were going to ruin; and not having been able to ſtrengthen them by abbatis, nor in any other manner than by a ſlight fraizing, which the enemy's artillery were demoliſhing wherever they fired, my opinion entirely coincided with that of the engineer and principal officers

of

of the army, that they were in many parts affailable in the forenoon, and that by the continuance of the fame fire for a few hours longer, they would be in fuch a flate as to render it defperate with our numbers to attempt to maintain them. We at that time could not fire a fingle gun; only one eight inch mortar and little more than one hundred cohorn fhells remained: a diverfion of the French fhips of war that lay at the mouth of the North river was to be expected; our numbers had been diminifhed by the enemy's fire, but particularly by ficknefs; and the ftrength and fpirits of thofe in the works were much exhaufted by the fatigue of conftant watching and unremitting duty. Under all thefe circumftances, I thought it would be wanton and inhuman to the laft degree to facrifice the lives of this fmall body of gallant foldiers, who had ever behaved with fo much fidelity and courage, by expofing them to an affault, which, from the numbers and precautions of the enemy, could not fail to fucceed. I therefore propofed to capitulate. The treatment in general that we have received from the enemy, fince our furrender, has been perfectly good and proper; but the kindnefs and attention that has been fhown to us by the French officers in particular, their delicate fenfibility of our fituation, their generous and preffing offers of money, both public and private, to any amount, has really gone beyond what I can poffibly defcribe, and will, I hope make an impreffion on the breaft of every Britifh officer, whenever the fortune of war fhould put any of them into our power.

Although the event has been fo unfortunate, the patience of the foldiers in bearing the greateft fatigues, and their firmnefs and intrepidity under a perfevering fire of fhot and fhells that I believe has not often been exceeded, deferves the higheft commendation and praife.

A fuccefsful defence in our fituation was perhaps impoffible, for the place could only be reckoned an intrenched camp, fubject in moft places to enfilade, and the ground in general fo difadvantageous, that nothing but the neceffity of fortifying it as a poft to protect the navy could have induced any perfon to erect works upon it; our force daily diminifhed by ficknefs, and other loffes, and was reduced, when we offered to capitulate, on this fide, to little more than 3,200 rank and file fit for duty, including officers, fervants, and artificers; and at Gloucefter about 600, including cavalry. The enemy's army confifted of upwards of 8000 French, nearly as many continentals, and 5000 militia. They brought an immenfe train of heavy artillery, moft amply furnifhed with ammunition, and perfectly well manned.

Lieutenant-Colonel Abercromby will have the honour to deliver this difpatch, and is well qualified to explain to your Excellency every particular relating to our paft and prefent fituation.

I have the honour to be, &c.

(Signed)　　　　　　　CORNWALLIS.

III. *General*

III. *General Washington's Farewell Letter, to each of the Go-*
vernors, of the Thirteen United States of America, contain-
ing his Monitions, and Opinion, concerning good and effectual
Government.—————— Being his Excellency's Legacy,
to his Countrymen.

Head Quarters, Newburgh, June 11, 1783.

SIR,

THE great object for which I had the honour to hold an ap-
pointment in the fervice of my country being accomplifhed,
I am now preparing to refign it into the hands of Congrefs, and to
return to that domeftic retirement, which it is well known, I left
with the greateft reluctance—a retirement for which I have never
ceafed to figh, through a long and painful abfence, and in which
(remote from the noife and trouble of the world) I meditate to pafs
the remainder of life in a ftate of undifturbed repofe : but before
I carry this refolution into effect, I think it a duty incumbent on
me, to make this my laft official communication—to congratulate
you on the glorious events which Heaven has been pleafed to produce in our favour : to offer my fentiments refpecting fome important fubjects, which appear to me to be intimately connected with
the tranquillity of the United States ; to take my leave of your Excellency as a public character ; and to give my final bleffing to
that country in whofe fervice I have fpent the prime of my life ; for
whofe fake I have confumed fo many anxious days and watchful
nights ; and whofe happinefs being extremely dear to me, will
always conftitute no inconfiderable part of my own.

Impreffed with the livelieft fenfibility on this pleafing occafion, I
will claim the indulgence of dilating the more copioufly on the fubject of our mutual felicitation. When we confider the magnitude of
the prize we contended for, the doubtful nature of the conteft, and
the favourable manner in which it has terminated, we fhall find
the greateft poffible reafon for gratitude and rejoicing : this is a
theme that will afford infinite delight to every benevolent and
liberal mind, whether the event in contemplation be confidered as
the fource of prefent enjoyment, or the parent of future happinefs ;
and we fhall have equal occafion to felicitate ourfelves on the lot
which Providence has affigned us whether we view it in a natural,
a political, or moral point of light.

The citizens of America, placed in the moft enviable condition,
as the fole lords and proprietors of a vaft tract of continent, com-
prehending all the various foils and climates of the world, and
abounding with all the neceffaries and conveniencies of life, are
now, by the late fatisfactory pacification, acknowledged to be poffeffed of abfolute freedom and independency : they are from this
period

period to be confidered as the actors on a moft confpicuous theatre, which feems to be peculiarly defignated by Providence for the difplay of human greatnefs and felicity. Here they are not only furrounded with every thing which can contribute to the completion of private and domeftic enjoyment, but Heaven has crowned all its other bleffings, by giving a fairer opportunity for political happinefs, than any other nation has ever been favoured with. Nothing can illuftrate thefe obfervations more forcibly, than a recollection of the happy conjuncture of times and circumftances under which our republic affumed its rank among the nations. The foundation of our empire was not laid in the gloomy age of ignorance and fuperftition, but at an epocha when the rights of mankind were better underftood and more clearly defined than at any former period ; the refearches of the human mind after focial happinefs have been carried to a great extent ; the treafures of knowledge, acquired by the labours of philofophers, fages and legiflators, through a long fucceffion of years, are laid open for our ufe, and their collected wifdom may be happily applied in the eftablifhment of our forms of government ; the free cultivation of letters, the unbounded extenfion of commerce, the progreffive refinement of manners, the growing liberality of fentiment, and above all, the pure and benign light of revelation, have had a meliorating influence on mankind, and encreafed the bleffings of fociety. At this aufpicious period, the United States came into exiftence as a nation, and if their citizens fhould not be compleatly free and happy, the fault will be entirely their own.

Such is our fituation, and fuch our are profpects ; but notwithftanding the cup of bleffing is thus reached out to us : notwithftanding happinefs is ours if we have a difpofition to feize the occafion and make it our own ; yet it appears to me, that there is an option ftill left to the United States of America, that it is in their choice, and depends upon their conduct, whether they will be refpectable and profperous, or contemptible and miferable as a nation, This is the time of their political probation : this is the moment when the eyes of the whole world are turned upon them : this is the moment to eftablifh or ruin their national character forever : this is the favourable moment to give fuch a tone to our fœderal government, as will enable it to anfwer the ends of its inftitution ; or this may be the ill-fated moment for relaxing the powers of the union, annihilating the cement of the confederation, and expofing us to become the fport of European politics, which may play one ftate againft another to prevent their growing importance, and to ferve their own interefted purpofes ; for, according to the fyftem of policy the ftates fhall adopt at this moment, they will ftand or fall ; and by their confirmation or lapfe it is yet to be decided, whether the revolution muft ultimately be confidered as a bleffing or a curfe —a bleffing or a curfe, not to the prefent age alone, for with our fate will the deftiny of unborn millions be involved.

With

With this conviction of the importance of the present crisis, silence in me would be a crime ; I will therefore speak to your Excellency the language of freedom and of sincerity without disguise ; I am aware, however, that those who differ from me in political sentiment may perhaps remark, I am stepping out of the proper line of my duty, and they may possibly ascribe to arrogance or ostentation, what I know is alone the result of the purest intention ; but the rectitude of my own heart, which disdains such unworthy motives, the part I have hitherto acted in life, the determination I have formed of not taking any share in public business hereafter, the ardent desire I feel, and shall continue to manifest, of quietly enjoying in private life, after all the toils of war, the benefits of a wise and liberal government, will, I flatter myself, sooner or later, convince my countrymen, that I could have no sinister views in delivering, with so little reserve, the opinions contained in this address.

There are four things which I humbly conceive are essential to the well being, I may even venture to say, to the existence of the United States as an independent power.

1st. An indissoluble union of the states under one fœderal head.

2dly. A sacred regard to public justice.

3dly. The adoption of a proper peace establishment. And,

4thly. The prevalence of that pacific and friendly disposition among the people of the United States, which will induce them to forget their local prejudices and policies, to make those mutual concessions which are requisite to the general prosperity, and in some instances, to sacrifice their individual advantages to the interests of the community.

These are the pillars on which the glorious fabric of our independency and national character must be supported : liberty is the basis ; and whoever would dare to sap the foundation or overturn the structure, under whatever specious pretexts he may attempt it, will merit the bitterest execrations and the severest punishment which can be inflicted by his injured country.

On the three first articles I will make a few observations, leaving the last to the good sense and serious consideration of those immediately concerned.

Under the first head, although it may not be necessary or proper for me in this place to enter into a particular disquisition of the principles of the union, and to take up the great question which has been frequently agitated, whether it be expedient and requisite for the states to delegate a larger proportion of power to Congress, or not— yet it will be a part of my duty and that of every true patriot, to assert without reserve, and to insist upon the following positions: that unless the states will suffer Congress to exercise those prerogatives they are undoubtedly invested with by the constitution, every thing must very rapidly tend to anarchy and confusion : that it is indispensible to the happiness of the individual states, that there should be lodged somewhere, a supreme power

power, to regulate and govern the general concerns of the confederated republic, without which the union cannot be of long duration; that there must be a faithful and pointed compliance on the part of every state, with the late proposals and demands of Congress, or the most fatal consequences will enfue; that whatever measures have a tendency to diffolve the union, or contribute to violate or leffen the fovereign authority, ought to be confidered as hostile to the liberty and independency of America, and the authors of them treated accordingly; and lastly, that unless we can be enabled, by the concurrence of the states, to participate of the fruits of the revolution, and enjoy the effential benefits of civil fociety, under a form of government fo free and uncorrupted, fo happily guarded against the danger of oppreffion, as has been devifed and adopted by the articles of confederation; that it will be a fubject of regret that fo much blood and treasure have been lavifhed for no purpofe, that fo many fufferings have been encountered without a compenfation, and that fo many facrifices have been made in vain. Many other confiderations might here be adduced to prove, that without an entire conformity to the fpirit of the union, we cannot exist as an independent power—it will be fufficient for my purpofe to mention but one or two which feem to me of the greatest importance: It is only in our united charadler as an empire, that our independence is acknowledged, that our power can be regarded, or our credit fupported among foreign nations. The treaties of the European powers with the United States of America, will have no validity on a diffolution of the union—we fhall be left nearly in a state of nature; or we may find by our own unhappy experience, that there is a natural and neceffary progreffion from the extreme of anarchy to the extreme of tyranny, and that arbitrary power is most eafily eftablifhed on the ruins of liberty abufed to licentioufnefs.

As to the fecond article which refpects the performance of public juftice, Congrefs have, in their late addrefs to the United States almost exhaufted the fubject: they have explained their ideas fo fully, and have enforced the obligations the states are under to render compleat juftice to all the public creditors, with fo much dignity and energy, that in my opinion no real friend to the honour and independency of America, can hefitate a fingle moment refpecting the propriety of complying with the just and honourable meafures propofed: if their arguments do not produce conviction, I know of nothing that will have greater influence; efpecially when we recollect, that the fyftem referred to, being the refult of the collected wifdom of the continent, must be efteemed if not perfect, certainly the least objedlionable of any that could be devifed, and that if it fhall not be carried into immediate execution, a national bankruptcy, with all its deplorable confequences, will take place before any different plan can poffibly be propofed and adopted. So preffing are the prefent circumftances! and fuch is the alternative now offered to the states!

O

The

The ability of the country to difcharge the debts which have been incurred in its defence, is not to be doubted— an inclination, I flatter myfelf, will not be wanting ; the path of our duty is plain before us : honefly will be found, on every experiment, to be the beft and only true policy ; let us, then, as a nation, be juft ; let us fulfil the public contracts, which Congrefs had undoubtedly a right to make for the purpofe of carrying on the war, with the fame good faith we fuppofe ourfelves bound to perform our private engagements: in the mean time let an attention to the chearful performance of their proper bufinefs as individuals and as members of fociety, be earneftly inculcated on the citizens of America ; then will they ftrengthen the hands of government, and be happy under its protection ; every one will reap the fruit of his labours ; every one will enjoy his own acquifitions without moleftation and without danger.

In this ftate of abfolute freedom and perfect fecurity, who will grudge to yield a very little of his property, to fupport the common interefts of fociety, and enfure the protection of government ? Who does not remember the frequent declarations at the commencement of the war, that we fhould be compleatly fatisfied, if at the expence of one half we could defend the remainder of our poffeffions ? Where is the man to be found who wifhes to remain indebted for the defence of his own perfon and property, to the exertions, the bravery, and the blood of others, without making one generous effort to repay the debt of honor and of gratitude ? In what part of the continent fhall we find any man, or body of men, who would not blufh to ftand up and propofe meafures purpofely calculated to rob the foldier of his ftipend, and the public creditor of his due ? And were it poffible that fuch a flagrant inftance of injuftice could ever happen, would it not excite the general indignation, and tend to bring down upon the authors of fuch meafures, the aggravated vengeance of Heave   If after all, a fpirit of difunion cr a temper of obftinacy and perverfenefs fhould manifeft itfelf in any of the ftates; if fuch an ungracious difpofition fhould attempt to fruftrate all the happy effects that might be expected to flow from the union : if there fhould be a refufal to comply with the requifitions for funds to difcharge the annual intereft of the public debts ; and if that refufal fhould revive again all thofe jealoufies, and produce all thofe evils which are now happily removed. Congrefs, who have in all their tranfactions fhewn a great degree of magnanimity and juftice, will ftand juftified in the fight of God and man: and the ftate alone which puts itfelf in oppofition to the aggregate wifdom of the continent, and follows fuch miftaken and pernicious councils, will be refponfible for all the confequences.

For my own part, confcious of having acted, while a fervant of the public, in the manner I conceived beft fuited to promote the real intereft of my country : having in confequence of my fixed belief, in fome meafure pledged myfelf to the army, that their country would finally do them compleat and ample juftice; and
not

not wishing to conceal any instance of my official conduct from the eyes of the world, I have thought proper to transmit to your Excellency the enclosed collection of papers, relative to the half pay and commutation granted by Congress to the officers of the army ; from these commutations, my decided sentiments will be clearly comprehended, together with the conclusive reasons which induced me, at an early period, to recommend the adoption of this measure in the most earnest and serious manner. As the proceedings of Congress, the army and myself, are open to all, and contain, in my opinion, sufficient information to remove the prejudices and errors which may have been entertained by any, I think it unnecessary to say any thing more, than just to observe that the resolutions of Congress now alluded to, are undoubtedly as absolutely binding upon the United States as the most solemn acts of confederation or legislation. As to the idea, which I am informed has in some instances prevailed, that the half-pay and commutation are to be regarded merely in the odious light of a pension ; it ought to be exploded forever—that provision should be viewed, as it really was, a reasonable compensation offered by Congress, at a time when they had nothing else to give, to the officer of the army for services then to be performed—it was the only means to prevent a total dereliction of the service ; it was a part of their hire, I may be allowed to say, it was the price of their blood and of your independency ; it is therefore more than a common debt ; it is a debt of honor ; it can never be considered as a pension or gratuity, nor be cancelled until it is fairly discharged.

With regard to a distinction between officers and soldiers, it is sufficient that the uniform experience of every nation of the world, combined with our own, proves the utility and propriety of the discrimination : rewards in proportion to the aids the public derives from them, are unquestionably due to all its servants. In some lines, the soldiers perhaps have generally had as ample a compensation for their services, by the large bounties which have been paid to them, as their officers will receive in the proposed commutation : in others, if besides the donation of lands, the payment of arrearages of cloathing and wages (in which articles all the component parts of the army must be put upon the same footing) we take into the estimate the bounties many of the soldiers have received and the gratuity of one year's full pay, which is promised to all, possibly their situation (every circumstance being duly considered) will not be deemed less eligible than that of the officers ; should a farther reward, however be judged equitable, I will venture to assert, no one will enjoy greater satisfaction than myself, on seeing an exemption from taxes for a limited time (which has been petitioned for in some instances) or any other adequate immunity or compensation, granted to the brave defenders of their country's cause : but neither the adoption or rejection of this proposition will in any manner affect, much less militate against the act of Congress, by

which

which they have offered five years full pay, in lieu of the half-pay
for life, which had been before promised to the officers of the army.
Before I conclude the subject of public justice, I cannot omit to
mention the obligations this country is under to that meritorious
class of veteran non-commissioned officers and privates who have
been discharged for inability, in consequence of the resolution of
Congress of the 23d of April 1782, on annual pension for life;
their peculiar sufferings, their singular merits and claims to that
provision, need only be known, to interest all the feelings of humanity in their behalf— nothing but a punctual payment of their
annual allowance can rescue them from the most complicated mifery—and nothing could be a more melancholy and distressing fight,
than to behold those who have shed their blood or lost their limbs
in the service of their country, without a shelter, without a friend,
and without the means of obtaining any of the necessaries or com-
forts of life, compelled to beg their daily bread from door to door!
Suffer me to recommend those of this description, belonging to
your state, to the warmest patronage of your excellency and your
legislature.

It is necessary to say but a few words on the third topic which
was proposed, and which regards particularly the defence of the
republic: as there can be little doubt but Congress will recommend
a proper peace establishment for the United-States, in which a due
attention will be paid to the importance of placing the militia of
the union upon a regular and respectable footing—if this should be
the case, I would beg leave to urge the great advantage of it in the
strongest terms: The militia of this country must be considered as
the palladium of our security and the first effectual resort in case of
hostility—it is essential, therefore, that the same system should
pervade the whole; that the formation and discipline of the militia
of the continent should be absolutely uniform, and that the same
species of arms, accoutrements and military apparatus, should be
introduced in every part of the United-States: No one who has
not learnt it from experience, can conceive the difficulty, expence
and confusion which result from a contrary system, or the vague
arrangements which have hitherto prevailed.

If in treating of political points, a greater latitude than usual
has been taken in the course of this address, the importance of
the crisis and the magnitude of the objects in discussion, must be
my apology: It is, however, neither my wish or expectation that
the preceding observations should claim any regard, except so far
as they shall appear to be dictated by a good intention, consonant
to the immutable rules of justice, calculated to produce a liberal
system of policy, and founded on whatever experience may have
been acquired by a long and close attention to public business:
here I might speak with the more confidence from my actual
observations, and if it would not swell this letter (already too prolix)
beyond the bounds I had prescribed myself, I could demonstrate to
every mind open to conviction, that in less time, and with much
                                                              less

less expence than has been incurred, the war might have been brought to the same happy conclusion, if the resources of the continent could have been properly brought forth; that the distresses and disappointments which have very often occurred, have, in too many instances, resulted more from a want of energy in the continental government, than a deficiency of means in the particular states; that the inefficacy of measures arising from the want of an adequate authority in the Supreme Power, from a partial compliance with the requisitions of Congress in some of the states, and from a failure of punctuality in others, while it tended to damp the zeal of those which were more willing to exert themselves, served also to accumulate the expences of the war, and to frustrate the best concerted plans; and that the discouragement occasioned by the complicated difficulties and embarrassments, in which our affairs were by this means involved, would have long ago produced the dissolution of any army, less patient, less virtuous, and less persevering than that which I have had the honor to command: But while I mention these things, which are notorious facts, as the defects of our fœderal constitution, particularly in the prosecution of a war, I beg it may be understood, that as I have ever taken a pleasure in gratefully acknowledging the assistance and support I have derived from every class of citizens, so shall I always be happy to do justice to the unparalleled exertions of the individual states on many interesting occasions.

I have thus freely disclosed what I wished to make known before I surrendered up my public trust to those who committed it to me. The task is now accomplished. I now bid adieu to your Excellency as the chief magistrate of your state; at the same time I bid a last farewell to the cares of office and all the employments of public life. It remains then to be my final and only request, that your Excellency will communicate these sentiments to your legislature at their next meeting, and that they may be considered as the legacy of one who has ardently wished, on all occasions, to be useful to his country, and who, even in the shade of retirement, will not fail to implore the divine benediction upon it.

I now make it my earnest prayer, that God would have you, and the state over which you preside, in his holy protection; that he would incline the hearts of the citizens to cultivate a spirit of subordination and obedience to government; to entertain a brotherly affection and love for one another, for their fellow citizens of the United States at large, and particularly for their brethren who have served in the field; and finally, that he would most graciously be pleased to dispose us all, to do justice, to love mercy, and to demean ourselves with that charity, humility, and pacific temper of mind, which were the characteristics of the divine author of our blessed religion, and without an humble imitation of whose example in these things, we can never hope to be a happy nation.

I have the honour to be, with esteem and regard, Sir, your Excellency's most obedient servant,

G. WASHINGTON.

CONSIDERATIONS on the PEACE:

Extracted from the POLITICAL MAGAZINE,
*Printed in London—*1783.

The British Minister has by the late Peace made the following national conceſſions.

To the AMERICANS.

THE entire, abſolute, and ſovereign independence of New-Hampſhire, Maſſachuſets-Bay, Rhode-Iſland, and Providence Plantations. Connecticut, New-York. New-Jerſey, Penſylvania, Delaware, Maryland, Virginia, North-Carolina, South-Carolina, and Georgia, with *all Iſlands within twenty leagues of any part of the ſhores of the ſaid United States.*

A full and ample participation of the fiſheries on the Banks of Newfoundland, in the Gulf of St. Laurence, and at all other *places in the ſea* where the inhabitants of both countries uſed at any time heretofore to fiſh ; as alſo on the coaſts, bays and creeks of all other his Britannick Majeſty's dominions in America. with *liberty to dry and cure fiſh* in any of the *unſettled bays, harbours, and creeks of Nova-Scotia, Magdalen Iſlands, and Labradore.*

An evacuation *with all convenient ſpeed, and without cauſing any deſtruction or carrying away any negroes or other property,* of every *port, place, and harbour* within the ſaid United States.

A relinquiſhment, and leaving behind in all fortifications the American artillery that may be therein.

A reſtoration of all archives, records, deeds, and papers belonging to any of the ſaid States or their citizens, to be *forthwith* delivered to the proper ſtate and perſon to whom they may belong.

GREAT BRITAIN receives in compenſation for all the foregoing conceſſions:

From the AMERICANS.

An earneſt *recommendation* from Congreſs to the *legiſlatures* of the *reſpective* States, to provide for the reſtitution of all eſtates, &c. that have been confiſcated belonging to *real* Britiſh ſubjects, and alſo of the eſtates, &c. of perſons, *(loyaliſts) reſident in diſtricts* in the poſſeſſion of his *Majeſty's arms,* and who have *not borne arms* againſt the United States, and that perſons *(loyaliſts)* of any other deſcription, ſhall have *free liberty to go to and remain in,* any of the *ſaid States* for twelve months, unmoleſted in their

endeavours

endeavours to *obtain the restitution* of such of their estates, &c. and that such restoration *shall be recommended* as aforesaid, to be made to such persons *(loyalists)* upon their *refunding* the *purchase money* paid since the confiscation by the present possessors.—*This is all.*

Besides the general reasons for Great Britain coming so unexpectedly to a treaty of pacification, the failure of the harvest, which threatened a famine, is particularly urged, as perhaps nothing but the supply of grain which the peace may enable us to draw from America could effectually prevent that awful event. Peace would have been worthily obtained by the cession of Gibraltar; it would have been saving an immense expence, and that too for an object now become insignificant——our Mediterranean trade. Yet the ministry are entitled to commendation for wisely yielding to the voice of the people in retaining it, whether that voice was judicious or not. Weakened, humbled, and on the brink of ruin, safety, not glory, was the principal object by which our statesmen were to be directed. The treaty with America is just and liberal. The Americans had it in contemplation to compose a book of all their sufferings, and to make it a school book for their children, and such an institution would have continued an evil spirit for ages; but since the acknowledgement of Independency, and the peace, the design has been laid aside. Granting them Independency was nothing more than what in fact they had already obtained.

As to the limits, they are the only ones that could have been chosen without giving afterward occasion to much disorder and contention. The Canada furr trade will be in part affected, but that object was not so great as to merit a continuance of the war, and as to retaining the forts south of the British boundaries, such a treaty would have proved not so much a termination of the old, as the beginning of a new war.

Penobscot has not a tree left in it fit for a mast, and if the growing timber should hereafter be fit for masts, it may be purchased from the American freeholder, as well as if the land belonged to British subjects.

Concerning the Canada boundaries, government had two views; one political, a permanent peace; to obtain which, it was necessary to prevent every ground of future jealousy; the other view was commercial; monopolies begin to be exploded, and to have contended about a few furrs, would have been incompatible with a design of such a magnitude and importance, as an enlarged plan of commerce.——And with regard to the fishery, if a share had not been granted the Americans, they would have stolen in upon us, in spite of all our endeavours, and we should have been involved in endless altercations with them.

Measurement of the countries ceded in America.

Many people are unable to form an adequate idea of the extent of the district ceded in America, because the geography of that immense country is not well known. It will not be amiss therefore to
compare

compare the diftricts ceded, with the countries with which we are
more acquainted. The following measurements are made with
accuracy.

The river Ohio is navigable from Fort Pitt to its mouth, which
is a length of 1164 miles.—

The lands on the banks of the Ohio, and between the Allegany
Mountains, the lakes Ontario and Erie, and the Illinois and
Mississippi rivers, contain 233,200 square miles, which is nearly
equal to Great Britain and France, whose contents are only
235,237 square miles:—

The lands between the Illinois, Lakes Huron and Superior,
and the Mississippi at the Falls of St. Anthony, contain 129,030
square miles, nearly equal to Great Britain and Ireland, which
contain only 131,800 square miles.

The lands from St. Anthony's Falls to the South line from the
Lake of the woods to the head of the Mississippi, contain 50,000
square miles, which is more than all Holland, Flanders and Ireland, which contain only 57,098 square miles.

East Florida alone contains 35,000 square miles, and is nearly
as large as Ireland, which has only 35,400 square miles—

The United States of America contain 207,050 square miles,
nearly as large as all Germany, Flanders, Holland, and Switzerland, which contain 207,483 square miles.

NEW PUBLICATIONS, at BELL's
Book-Store, near St. Paul's Church, in Third Street, Philadelphia.

I. Moore's View of Society and Manners, in France, Switzerland,
Germany, and Italy: *Being the very celebrated Travels of the
said Dr. Moore, of Glasgow, which he performed in the years,
1775, 1776, 1777, and 1778, in company with his Grace the
present Duke of Hamilton,* four volumes compleat in two. *At
the small price of Four Dollars.*

II. The Adventures of an East-Indian RUPEE; wherein are In-
terspersed various Anecdotes, ASIATIC and EUROPEAN.
Price Half a Dollar.

III. Sermons to Ministers of State, political, philosophical, and
religious, by the author of Sermons to Asses, and to Doctors in
Divinity, *Price Half a Dollar.*

IV. Emma Corbett, exhibiting, Henry and Emma, the faithful
modern Lovers, as delineated by themselves, in their original
Letters.——— *In this admirable Work, the power of Love, and
the miseries of War, are feelingly depicted; founded upon Incidents,
which occurred at and near Philadelphia, in the* ROYAL WINTER,
of 1777, *when the* BRITISH GENTRY, *imagined they had taken
an eternal Lease of the great Congressional City.* To which is
added, THE MAN OF FEELING, *in neat Binding. Two Dollars.*

V. The Man of the World, by Mr. Mackenzie.—To which are
added— Lord Lyttelton's Letters and Poems. *Price two Dollars.*